Tales From the Tribe Dugout

By Russell Schneider

Sports Publishing LLC
www.sportspublishingllc.com

Director of production: Susan M. Moyer
Dust jacket design:Kenneth O'Brien
Interior art: Tom Denny

ISBN:1-58261-303-6

Printed in the United States of America

Sports Publishing LLC
www.sportspublishingllc.com

This book is dedicated to my wife Catherine, whose patience, understanding, support and encouragement over the years have been a blessing and, as with my previous nine books, deservedly shares whatever success "Tales from the Tribe Dugout" achieves ...

And to my late mother, Maybelle, the greatest and most unwavering Tribe fan I ever knew, and to my late father, Robert, who eventually came to appreciate baseball because his wife and son were so completely addicted to the game ...

And to the players, managers, coaches and executives whose "tales" are related on the following pages ...

And to Baseball itself, a most wonderful game that has survived so much, from within its ranks, as without ...

And to the fans who love the game—and the Tribe.

—Russell Schneider
Cleveland, Ohio
December 2001

Acknowledgments

There are many whose assistance and cooperation I gratefully acknowledge in the preparation and development of *Tales from the Tribe Dugout*, as well as the nine books that preceded it, and also those who helped make my career as a sportswriter truly a labor of love, beginning at the beginning with Gordon Cobbledick, the late sports editor of the *Plain Dealer*, who hired me in 1964 to cover the Cleveland Indians; his successor and my friend, Hal Lebovitz; other colleagues and competitors during, and since those great (and sometimes not-so-great) days covering the Tribe and then the Cleveland Browns, including Chuck Heaton, Bob August, Dick Zunt, Hank Kozloski, Bob Sudyk, the late Jim Schlemmer, Paul Hoynes, Burt Graeff, Jim Ingraham and Sheldon Ocker; other friends in, and of the media, namely Dino Lucarelli, Bob DiBiasio, Bart Swain, Curtis Danburg, John Krepop and Joe Corrado; certainly (most) members of the Indians players, managers, coaches and executives whose wonderful stories and anecdotes fill the following pages; Tom Denny, for his exceptional artwork; and Mike Pearson, who presented the opportunity for this book to be written, and Susan M. Moyer, Kenny O'Brien, and others at Sports Publishing, Inc. for their editorial and design contributions.

Thanks again.

Contents

Maw June 2

Introduction

It was late February, 1964, when the rookie baseball writer for *The Plain Dealer* nervously drove into the parking lot at Hi Corbett Field in Tucson, Arizona. The Cleveland Indians were about to start spring training for what they hoped would be a return to glory, in this case a 10-year return to glory, as they had not won the pennant since 1954.

As I walked onto the field and waited for the players to come out of the clubhouse, my boss, Gordon Cobbledick, the courtly and *usually* distinguished-looking sports editor of *The Plain Dealer*, already was there, though I hardly recognized him.

"Cobby," as everyone called him, was wearing a western shirt, string tie with a scorpion clasp, jeans and boots, and looked more like a grizzled cowpoke than the dignified sports editor of one of America's leading newspapers.

Gesturing toward my sport coat, white shirt and tie, Cobby said, not unpleasantly but nonetheless sternly, "We don't dress that way . . . not here . . . not now." Then, with a patient smile he told me, "Go back to the hotel and get rid of that coat and tie. You don't need them. Not here. Not now," he said again.

Which was my indoctrination to the best job—OK, the *second best* job—and career I'd ever wanted. (The first was to be playing the game, instead of writing about it. This was after I'd learned that a major league curve ball was much more difficult to hit than one thrown on the sandlots, or even at the Class D minor league level.)

Much has happened in the four decades since that indoctrination—since two rookie pitchers, Sam McDowell and Tommy John, and three hot-shot young position players named Max Alvis, Tony Martinez and Vic Davalillo, were expected to form the cornerstone of a dynasty that would bring many pennants to Cleveland.

They didn't, of course, although in the years that followed, while the Indians seldom—until recently—resembled a pennant contender, there has been no shortage of interesting players (OK, even *characters*), many of whose stories comprise this book.

Also in the years that followed that late February morning in Tucson, while it took the Indians 41 seasons, until 1995, to win another pennant, their fourth in what was then the 95-year history of the American League, more bad baseball was played along the shores of Lake Erie than good.

But the franchise always prevailed and survived, despite numerous instances of mismanagement, severe financial instability, some capricious trades, serious injuries—even the deaths of several star players—and other emergencies and crises, including player strikes and owner lockouts.

Baseball has survived, too—and certainly *hopefully*—it always will. It is the greatest, most challenging and perfect game ever invented and, from my perspective, a career spent covering baseball is second best only to playing it.

Also, from my perspective, little has changed since that morning in Tucson four decades ago—with one exception.

Now, nobody needs to tell me, as Cobby did back then, to get rid of the coat and tie. Especially the tie.

Joe Adcock

(First baseman, 1963; Manager, 1967)

On Opening Day, 1967, Joe Adcock's first—and only —season as a major league manager, the Indians played the Athletics, who were then based in Kansas City. The A's were owned by flamboyant Charles O. Finley, who introduced to baseball what he called "wedding gown white" uniforms trimmed in green and gold.

Finley's players also wore white shoes, which was another drastic style change. Until then professional baseball teams wore black spikes.

So when "Jumbo Jim" Nash took the mound and made his first pitch, Adcock bolted out of the Indians dugout, complaining to umpire Larry Napp that the pitcher's white shoes were "distracting" the Tribe batters. Maybe they did, as Kansas City won, 4-3, with the Indians getting only five hits off Nash.

Adcock formally protested the loss, citing the distraction of Nash's white shoes, but it was disallowed by then-American League president Joe Cronin.

Among Adcock's problems was his inability to deal with the media. Early on, when asked by a sportswriter if he thought a certain umpire blew a call against the Indians, he replied, "Does a bear [defecate] in the woods?" which, thereafter, became his standard response to questions he chose to avoid answering.

Robbie Alomar

(Second baseman, 1999-)

"Even though my brother Sandy is playing for the Chicago White Sox, we stay in touch regularly. We talk on the phone a couple of times a week, although I'm usually the one who does the calling. Sandy always tells me that I should be calling him, because I make more money."

Upon joining the Indians in 1999, Robbie said, "I'm not only a player of the game, I'm a student of the game. I watch and learn," to which Jack McKeon, Alomar's former manager (San Diego Padres) commented, "You never had to tell Robbie Alomar a thing. He always knew what to do."

Sandy Alomar, Jr.

(Catcher, 1990-95)

Upon his acquisition (with Carlos Baerga and Chris James for Joe Carter) from San Diego in 1990, Sandy Alomar played a prominent role in the Indians' resurgence in winning five consecutive American League Central Division championships.

After the Indians reached the postseason playoffs in 1995 for the first time in 41 years, clinching the A.L. Central title on September 8, 1995, Alomar said, "I cried, thinking of all we'd gone through to get to where we are."

Max Alvis

(Third baseman, 1962-69)

"Once, early in my career when my sons Max and Steve were very young, they were playing ball in the backyard and trying to identify with big leaguers. I heard Max say, 'I'm going to be Rocky Colavito,' and then David said, 'OK, I'll be Fred Whitfield.'

"I hollered out the window, 'Hey, you guys, why don't you want to be Max Alvis?' and one of them replied, 'Aw, dad, you strike out too much.'"

"Everybody knows that Chicago is called the 'Windy City,' but nobody knows it better than I do—from personal experience.

"We were playing the White Sox in Chicago (in 1966) and the wind caused me the greatest embarrassment of my baseball career. It was late in the game, we were in the field and a foul ball was popped up in my direction (third base). I backpedaled to get under it, but the wind started taking the ball out toward left field. The thought crossed my mind that the ball was drifting quite a bit, but I figured I was OK, because I was in foul territory.

"So I kept backpedaling and, just as I reached up to catch the ball, I tripped over third base and fell backwards. The back of my head hit the ground, and the ball landed a couple of feet away. It was still foul, but the batter got a life and subsequently got a hit. I was very embarrassed . . . and the fact that we lost the game made it worse.

"In a way—make that a couple of ways—it was kind of funny, as I found out later. While I was backpedaling to get under the ball, Herb Score, who was broadcasting the game on the radio, saw what was developing and was hollering into the microphone, 'Watch out for the bag! Watch out for the bag!' I know that because people in Cleveland who were listening to the game told me.

"Something else that's funny—now, but not then—is that Brownie (Larry Brown) was playing shortstop and (manager) Birdie Tebbetts jumped all over him for not backing me up and catching the ball himself. But to my face, Birdie just shook his head and said, 'Max, I've been in baseball 30 years and I've never seen anything like that. Never.' I never did either.

"But that still wasn't the end of it. After the game we flew to California to play the Angels. When I went out on the field for batting practice (Angels shortstop) Jim Fregosi saw me and flopped down on the ground and started rolling around, laughing. He told me, 'Max, that was the funniest thing I ever saw the first time, and it was even funnier on instant replay.'

"See, the game was on national television and, not only did they show it when it happened, they kept on replaying it."

Joe Azcue

(Catcher, 1963-69)

"When the Indians got me, I was playing at (Class AAA) Portland (in the Kansas City Athletics) farm system. I had started with Cincinnati, they traded me to Kansas City (in 1962). When spring training ended in 1963, they said they were sending me to Portland to get me in better shape because they were going to do some changing around. I joined the Portland team in Hawaii, which was very nice, and then I returned to Portland with the team.

"My wife and daughter Angela, who had just been born, met me there, and we got an apartment. A couple days later I was told, 'Joe, we traded you to the Indians, and you have to go to Cleveland right away.' I thought they were kidding. I said, 'Bull----. I just got here, so did my wife and baby. We just bought a car, and now I have to go to Cleveland?' Then I said it again. 'Bull----. I just got here, and I am not going to Cleveland.'

"But then (Indians general manager) Gabe Paul called me. He and (manager) Birdie Tebbetts knew me from when they were in Cincinnati and Gabe signed me, and I knew I had to go. So I flew all night—about seven hours in a propeller plane—with my wife and baby to Cleveland. I had to leave my car at the airport in Portland and ask a guy to sell it for me. We didn't know a soul in Cleveland, and we got there just in time for me to go to the ballpark for a doubleheader.

"The only person I knew on the team was Pedro Ramos. He let my wife and baby stay with his family because right after the double header, the Indians were leaving on a road trip. It was crazy. There's my wife with a brand

Joe Azcue

new baby and she doesn't know anybody in town. Isn't that amazing?

"When I got to the ballpark I told (coach) Mel Harder that I flew all night and did not get any sleep. He said, 'Why don't you just go out to the bullpen and take a nap. We won't use you unless we need you.'

"So I'm out in the bullpen sleeping, and in the fourth inning of the first game (catcher John) Romano got hit with a foul tip and broke his hand. They woke me up and said I had to go in the game to catch. I think it was either Gary Bell or Mudcat Grant who was pitching. I was still half asleep; I didn't know any of the pitchers, not even their names.

"But I had a great day. I hit a home run and got a couple more hits, and we won both games. With Romano hurt I was the only (healthy) catcher for almost a month. But I had a great season, and that's when somebody started calling me the 'Immortal Cuban.' The rest is history. I was making $8,500 that season, which was a lot of money then, and I was very happy with it."

"Here's what it was like to catch Sam McDowell, how he always wanted to call his own pitches. He'd brush up or down with his glove against his uniform shirt to add or subtract from the number I would give him. Sometimes he would cross himself up—not just me, but himself. I don't know why. Maybe because he didn't know how to add or subtract.

"A lot of times I didn't know what Sam was going to throw, and I would tell the umpire and the hitter that I didn't. They would say, 'What! Are you crazy or something?' I'd say, 'No, I'm serious,' and the hitter would say, 'Aw, come on,' and I would say again, 'No, really. I don't know.' Maybe that helped Sam. I don't know.

"Sometimes, when I didn't know what was coming, I'd just duck and the ball would go back to the backstop. When that would happen, Sam would call me out to the mound and I'd yell to him, 'No, no, you come here,' and the umpire would get mad and say, 'You guys better get together.'

"That was Sam. But he was a helluva pitcher. The best left-hander I ever caught."

"Let me tell you about (manager) Birdie Tebbetts. Anytime somebody on the team would say that famous big word, you know, the four letter one that starts with an 'F,' Birdie would fine him $50. And if we used the famous big word with 'mother' in front of it, it would cost us twice as much, $100. So what we did, we changed it around and instead of saying the words, we'd call somebody, 'Hey, you two big words,' and Birdie couldn't fine us.

"One time in Chicago a guy was ragging on me. I got mad and yelled to him, 'Hey, shut up you mother . . . you know.' But before I could finish it, Birdie stopped me and said, 'Joe, it'll cost you a hundred to finish it. But I was so mad at the guy, I said to Birdie, 'That's OK. Put me down for two hundred,' and I called the guy those two big words twice.

"After the game Birdie called me into his office and said, 'Joe, my son, be a professional. Don't say things like that,' and after that I didn't."

Scott Bailes

(Pitcher, 1986-89)

"People don't realize it, but because of the Indians, I made my acting debut in a 1987 movie. It was when Hollywood was filming *Major League*, the movie about the Indians, and how hapless they were. Most of the filming was done at Milwaukee County Stadium, but a couple of times they shot overhead scenes from a helicopter at our Stadium in Cleveland. I think it was either Opening Day or July 4, because those were two of the few dates we were expected to have a large crowd.

"We were told by the director that he wanted to see just the crowd, and we (players) were to go off the field and stay in the dugouts until we were told to come running out on the field. When the helicopter came overhead (pitcher) Jamie Easterly said, 'Scottie, here's your chance . . . you've got to be in this scene.' So I jumped up in the bullpen and, if you watch that part of the movie real close, you'll see a guy in the bullpen waving his arms like crazy.

"It was me. That was my acting debut—though it didn't lead to anything. I never got any more parts."

"In 1986 we had some older guys on the team (pitchers) Steve Carlton and Phil Niekro, and a bunch of rookies —Andy Allanson, Cory Snyder, Greg Swindell, and me. Allanson was the regular catcher and even though he was young, he was a real take-charge guy. A lot of the veteran pitchers didn't like him yelling at them, especially Carlton and Niekro, and who could blame them? After all, they were headed for the Hall of Fame.

"When we went into New York the first time (manager) Pat Corrales gave us rookies advice as to where not to go in the city, and that we'd be better off staying close to the hotel. He also emphasized that we shouldn't try to stay up as late as everybody else does in New York . . . basically that we should get our sleep, that kind of stuff.

"But when Saturday night rolled around, Allanson, who figured he wouldn't be catching the next day, stayed out most of the night, until real late.

"That was about the time baseball was starting to do advance filming, and if the Indians could get another team's game on television, they'd tape it to study it later. So what happened? Our game that Sunday was nationally televised—I think it was the first time a Cleveland game was ever nationally televised—and during it the cameras panned our bullpen. There was Allanson, sleeping after his big Saturday night out in New York. Not only did the camera see him once, it came back and zoomed in on him, showed him down on the ground, his hat over his face, dead asleep during the game against the Yankees.

"Naturally it got back to the front office—Dan O'Brien was the general manager then—and he gave all of us a lot of hell about sleeping in the bullpen, which gave the veteran pitchers even more reason to get all over Andy's butt."

Len Barker

(Pitcher, 1979-83)

"A week or so before I pitched my perfect game (May 15, 1981), we were playing the Blue Jays in Toronto and

Bert Blyleven was pitching. He had a no-hitter going for eight innings, and when the (last half of the) ninth began, Dave Garcia, our manager, took Joe Charboneau out of left field and put Larry Littleton in for defense. So what happens? The first ball hit to left field—a catchable ball—Littleton lost it in the lights, or whatever, and it fell for a double, which turned out to be the only hit off Blyleven.

"The following week we were playing Toronto again, this time in Cleveland, and I had the perfect game going for eight innings. Between innings, while we were batting, I felt like I had the plague. Once I sat down next to (manager) Dave Garcia and he got up and walked away without saying a word. Then, before I went out for the ninth, Garcia came over to me and said, 'You want me to take Joe (Charboneau) out of left field and put Larry (Littleton) in for defense?' He was serious, and I immediately thought about what happened a week earlier in Toronto.

"I said to Dave, 'If you take out Joe, take me out, too.' I remembered how Littleton screwed up Blyleven's no-hitter. So Garcia didn't take Joe out of the game, though he wouldn't have gotten a chance to screw it up anyway. I got the first two batters, and then Ernie Whitt, a pinch hitter, was the last one. He hit a routine fly to center, and I knew it was over because Rick Manning was out there—not Littleton."

Gene Bearden

(Pitcher, 1947-50)

As a rookie left-hander, Gene Bearden pitched—and won—perhaps the single-most important game in the Indians' first 100 years. He beat the Red Sox, 8-3, in Boston's Fenway Park, with a five-hitter in an unprecedented, one-game playoff for the pennant in 1948 for his 20th victory of the season.

Then Bearden went on to win the third game of the World Series, beating the Boston Braves, 2-0, and three days later, working in relief of Bob Lemon, saved the Indians' 4-3 victory in the deciding sixth game.

Bearden threw all the standard pitches—fastball, curve, slider, change-up—though there were two others that might have contributed more heavily to his success, at least in 1948. That was the only one of his seven major league seasons in which he won more than eight games.

"I had a pretty good spitball," he later confessed, "though my knuckleball was my best pitch. It was the knuckleball that got me where I went. It had a downward rotation that made the ball drop when it got to the plate."

Comparing the way the game was played during his career (1947-53), Bearden said, "Times are so different now. If you're a pitcher, you can't pitch inside, or the batters will come out after you. They also did in my day, though they never got far, because Mr. Hegan (Tribe catcher Jim Hegan) would stop them before they got halfway.

Gene Bearden

"One who tried was Dave Philley (an outfielder who played for the White Sox in 1948, and became a member of the Indians in 1954). Mr. Philley didn't like it that I was pitching him tight and started out (to the mound), but he didn't make it. Mr. Hegan made sure of that."

Bearden had pitched Philley "tight"—or as he subsequently admitted, even tighter—to "protect" Larry Doby who, as the American League's first black player in 1947, was the target of much verbal abuse by opposing players.

"I had thrown the ball tighter than tight to Mr. Philley, actually behind him, and I guarantee it wasn't a knuckleball either. That's the way we protected Larry against the guys who gave him a bad time. They usually got the message. If they didn't the first time, we kept sending it to them.

"There were a few who were pretty bad in St. Louis, Bob Dillinger and Al Zarilla in particular. But we handled them in our own way. We threw behind them. Sometimes even between their legs."

It was a well-known fact that Boudreau and Indians vice president Hank Greenberg were not on the best of terms in 1948, and team owner Bill Veeck, of course, usually sided with Greenberg. Prior to the playoff game in Boston against the Red Sox, Bearden overheard Boudreau arguing with Greenberg and Veeck as he walked through the dugout to go to the bullpen to warm up.

"They (Veeck and Greenberg) were raising hell with Lou because he was going to play (outfielder) Allie Clark at first base. I don't think they were mad because I was pitching; it's just that they wanted Eddie Robinson to play first base.

"Finally I heard Lou say, '(Clark) is going to play first base . . . you can fire me if you want, but it will have to be after the game,' and that's the way it was left.

"Something else I'll never forget was what Clark said to me before I made my first pitch: 'Don't you dare throw over here and try to pick somebody off. Remember—I never played first base before.'

"I was crazy about Bill (Veeck), but I didn't have that same opinion of Greenberg. I never argued with him. . . . I just tell people what I think. What I told Greenberg (during contract negotiations in 1950) was that everybody couldn't be a Hall of Famer like he was, and that he ought to learn how to treat people. That was it. Just a clash of personalities between him and me."

Buddy Bell

(Third baseman/outfielder, 1972-78)

"When I took this job with the Rockies (as manager in 2000), I wanted to hire Dave Garcia, because he'd been around so long and had seen everything there is to see in baseball. I loved him when he was a coach for us in Cleveland.

"I had trouble reaching him by telephone, and when I finally did, I told him, 'Dave, this is Buddy Bell. I'm going to manage the Rockies, and I want you to come with me.' Dave said, 'What! Buddy, do you realize I'm 79 years old!' I told him, 'I don't want you to play second base, I want you as a coach.'"

Garcia accepted the job.

Gary Bell

(Pitcher, 1958-67)

"One of my favorite games was against the Boston Red Sox in Cleveland in 1958 or 1959, and every time I see Bill Monboquette he reminds me about it. He pitched against me that day. We were ahead, 1-0, going into the ninth inning, and up to then I'd struck out Ted Williams three times in a row. Pete Runnels was the leadoff hitter in the ninth, and while he was up at the plate getting ready to hit, Williams was stalking around in the dugout and looking out at me kind of weird. It scared the hell out of me.

"Runnels got a hit to bring up Williams, and as he dug in at the plate, he was still glaring at me. I was thinking that I'd just blow his big ass away again.

"But this time he hit a ball that made it to the upper deck of the old Stadium, which was a helluva long way, and the Red Sox won, 2-1. Somebody said I should have chased him around the bases. I didn't. . . . I respected him too much.

"Besides, I was afraid he'd come after me and hit me—not the ball—again."

"Before I was traded (in 1967) to Boston, I played for Joe Adcock (then the rookie manager of the Indians). We were in spring training that season, and after playing a game in Palm Springs we were going to Holtville (California) for another exhibition game the next day. The team bus was scheduled to leave at 10 o'clock in the morning.

"So, right after breakfast a couple of us came out of the hotel and were walking toward the bus—it was just going on 10 o'clock and we were only like 10 or 15 feet away from it—and Joe had the bus driver slam the door and take off.

"There we were, almost ready to get aboard, and he left us standing there. We had to rent a car to get to Holtville, which I guess was about 100 miles away. I never asked him why he did it; I just figured he was a big jerk.

"Another time, when Adcock was still playing for us (1963), we were in a game against the Red Sox, and Joe went up to hit against Dick Radatz, who was then in his prime. They called him 'The Monster,' because he was so big and threw so hard.

"Adcock stepped in to the batter's box, and Radatz threw him three 500 mph pieces of cheese (fastballs). Adcock never took the bat off his shoulder (and was called out on strikes). When he came back to the dugout he said, 'A fly landed on my bat and I couldn't pull the trigger.' He was serious! Just about everybody in the dugout fell on the ground laughing."

Jim Bibby

(Pitcher, 1975-77)

"After I was traded to Cleveland (from Texas, June 13, 1975) I had an incentive bonus clause in my 1977 contract that said if I started 30 games I'd get an additional ten grand.

Jeff Torborg was the manager then, and going into the latter part of the season, I had 29 starts when they wanted me to go to the bullpen and pitch in relief. Jeff asked me about doing it, because he said they didn't want to put their young kids in with the games on the line. I agreed when he assured me I'd get my 30th start, which I did, but not until the last day of the season when we were in Toronto. We were snowed out the first two days, and the third was a double header that ended the season.

"I started the first game and had a one-hitter for six innings, then they took me out. After I went home I kept waiting for my bonus to come, but it never did. Finally my lawyer called the Indians and told them it was time to pay me. I don't remember the exact date it was due, just that it was sometime after the season ended. But even after my lawyer called the Indians, they still didn't send the check. We waited another month or so, and my lawyer called them and said we were going to file for free agency.

"Just like that (general manager) Phil Seghi sent the money, but we already had filed a grievance. Phil claimed he had talked to my lawyer and told him that the Indians didn't have much money, and that my lawyer said not to worry about it, that they could wait until they had more money. But that conversation never took place.

"We met with the arbitrator during spring training (in 1978), and he ruled that the Indians had committed a breach of contract, and made me a free agent. I also was able to keep the $10,000 that they had finally sent me.

"As it turned out, the fact that the Indians defaulted on my contract was the best thing that ever happened to my career. After the arbitrator made me a free agent, I signed with Pittsburgh, which scored a lot of runs for me—not like Cleveland or Texas—and got me a World Series ring (in 1979)."

Bert Blyleven

(Pitcher, 1981-85)

"Sure, I knew I had a no-hitter going (in Toronto, May 6, 1981)," said Bert Blyleven. "Anytime you get through, oh, six innings without giving up a hit, you know you're working on one. And if you aren't aware of it, all you have to do is pay attention to your teammates. You get the silent treatment from them. Like Lenny (Barker) says, they treat you like you've got the plague, they don't want to do anything to jinx you."

Blyleven's near no-hitter was spoiled in the ninth when the first batter lined a "catchable" ball that was lost in the lights by left fielder Larry Littleton, who had entered the game that inning as a defensive replacement.

"My immediate reaction, of course, was dejection. The ball that Littleton missed hit him in the glove. He came in for it, and I could see by his reactions that he lost it in the lights. Remember, it was in the old ball park in Toronto, Exhibition Stadium, not Skydome. Maybe if Skydome had been built by then, it might have been different. But, hey, you can lose a ball in the sun, even in the roof at the Metrodome in Minneapolis. Besides, I wasn't the first guy to lose a no-hitter after going that far.

"Littleton apologized, and I told him not to worry about it, those things happen. What else could I say? I felt sorry for the guy. He tried. Sometimes we as pitchers tend to forget all the great plays that are made behind us. You have to take the good with the bad.

"What really bothered me was that after I got the next two guys out, George Bell hit a pretty good curve ball for a base hit, so not only had I lost my no-hitter, I also lost my shutout, though we won the game, 4-1."

It would have been Blyleven's second no-hitter. When he pitched for the Texas Rangers in 1977, he hurled a no-hit, 6-0 victory over California on September 22.

Alva T. "Ted" Bonda

(Indians General Partner/President, 1975-78)

"I had to chuckle when I read that Larry Dolan bought the Indians (November 4, 1999 for a reported $323 million) because I'll never forget the day that Armond Arnson and I tried to give the franchise away.

"Yes, I said we 'tried' to give the franchise away. It happened during what you guys in the media like to call the "bad old days," which—though I hate to admit it—is very close to being accurate.

"It was during 1977 when things were going badly on the field and at the box office. Especially at the box office. We needed money to operate, to pay the bills, and Armond and I went to the bank and asked for a loan. Actually, a loan on top of the loan we already had with the bank.

"Before we went in, Armond, who was one of our partners, asked me for the keys to our offices at the Stadium. I asked him why, and he said, 'You'll see,' which I soon did.

"We met with the president of the bank, asked for more money, and were turned down. We already owed them too much, he said.

"With that, Armond said thanks and we got up to leave. Then, suddenly, he turned back and said, 'Oh, by the way, you're going to need these,' and tossed the keys to our of-fices on the desk. 'Now the bank owns the Indians,' he said.

"Which was all the banker needed. He invited us to sit down and talk some more. We did and, not surprisingly, the bank didn't want to take over ownership of the Indians, and we got the loan.

"That's why I had to chuckle when Dolan paid all that money for the club."

Frank Robinson became baseball's first black manager on October 3, 1975, when he was hired by the Indians, and exactly two years, eight months and 19 days later—on June 19, 1977—he became baseball's first black manager to be fired.

"It (Robinson being fired) would have happened much sooner if (general manager) Phil Seghi had his way," Bonda said. "I hired Robinson, because I thought it was the right thing to do. It was time (for an African-American to man-age in the major leagues). And when Phil wanted to replace him (in mid-May, 1977) I refused to do so, because I didn't think it was the right thing to do.

"I wanted to keep Frank, but eventually I caved in to too many pressures, from the media and the fans, as well as from my associates" (meaning Seghi).

Ray Boone

(Shortstop/third baseman, 1948-53)

As a minor league shortstop in the Indians farm sys-tem after being converted from a catcher in 1947, Ray Boone was promoted to Cleveland in the final month of the 1948 season. "That was a working man's team, a bunch of blue-collar guys," he said of the Indians. "Some (of the veterans) had a lot of mileage on them, but they were all pros. Nobody had an ego, not even the guys who should have, like (Ken) Keltner and (Joe) Gordon, not even (Bob) Feller, and certainly not (Bob) Lemon.

"Back then, in spring training (in 1948), not many guys—maybe not anybody—thought we could win the pennant for one simple reason: nobody knew Gene Bearden was going to be a 20-game winner."

Boone also remembered how the Indians celebrated after they won the playoff game for the pennant and would open the World Series two days later against the National League champion Braves in Boston.

"Oh, man! The party we had was really something. When we showed up for the workout the next day, you wouldn't believe how hungover some of the guys were. (Manager) Lou Boudreau came into the clubhouse and said, 'There are three cabs waiting outside . . . you, you and you, get into one . . . you, you and you get into another . . . and you, you and you take the third one. Get over to the spa and sweat out the booze.'"

Dick Bosman

(Pitcher, 1973-75)

"I've made that play hundreds of times. It's an easy play. You take a couple of steps to your right, grab the ball, turn to the left, and just sort of flip it sidearm to first base.

"But that night it sailed right over (first baseman) Tom McCraw's head and cost me a perfect game (which would have been only the eighth in modern major league history at that point).

"Sure, it (a perfect game) would have been great, but it was still a no-hitter (4-0 over Oakland on July 19, 1974). I'm sorry I made the error, but hey, it was only the fourth inning, and nobody was thinking about a no-hitter, let alone a perfect game at that point. I know I wasn't. I just wanted to win the game."

Lou Boudreau

(Shortstop, 1938-50; Manager, 1942-50)

On November 24, 1941, at the age of 24 years, four months, and seven days, Lou Boudreau became major league baseball's youngest manager. He was given a two-year contract to play shortstop and pilot the team, replacing Roger Peckinpaugh, who moved into the front office as vice president of the Indians.

Boudreau's inexperience became evident almost immediately. On the first day of spring training, then at Ft. Myers, Florida, the "boy manager," as he was called, met with the writers covering the Indians and made an odd request.

"Fellows, I'd like to suggest that, in the future, you gentlemen show me your stories before they go into the papers, so that nothing will be written that might hurt our chances of winning."

Lou Boudreau

Gordon Cobbledick, then the baseball writer for the *Cleveland Plain Dealer*, told Boudreau, "Lou, we work for our newspapers, not for you or the Indians. You can run the team, but don't try to tell us how to write our stories."

In 1947, Boudreau, who'd grown tired of the Indians losing to the Boston Red Sox because of Ted Williams, devised the unique "Boudreau Shift" (also was called the "Williams Shift"). Only the third baseman covered the left side of the infield, with the left fielder virtually in center field. The object was to invite Williams to try to hit the ball to left.

"I knew Williams, and I knew his thoughts were on being the greatest hitter in the game of baseball," Boudreau explained. "I also knew Ted's disposition. It was important to him to face up to a challenge, and to beat it, when hitting was involved."

The shift was unveiled in the second game of a double header in Boston on July 14 (after Williams went 4-for-5 with three homers, all to right field, and drove in eight runs to help the Red Sox win the opener). When Williams saw how the Indians were deployed, he turned to umpire Bill Summers and said, "What the hell is going on? They can't do that."

But Summers told Williams, "As long as they have nine guys on the field, and eight of them are inside the foul lines, they can play anywhere they please."

Williams, as stubborn as he was good, seldom challenged the shift and, according to Boudreau at the end of the season, "Our charts showed that we were 37 percent more successful when we used the shift against Williams than when we didn't."

Several years later, after both were retired—and both enshrined in the Hall of Fame—Williams said of Boudreau: "He came the closest to being the most complete player of anyone I've ever seen in the game. Boudreau was a great hitter, a great shortstop, and a great manager."

An inspirational player-manager, partly because of his remarkable ability as a shortstop and hitter, Boudreau delivered what was one of the most important hits in the history of the franchise on August 8, 1948. It was in the opener of a crucial doubleheader against the New York Yankees. At the time, the Indians' record was 58-39, and they were in a virtual tie for first place with the Yankees and Philadelphia Athletics.

Boudreau had been sidelined, nursing an assortment of injuries—a contusion of the right shoulder, a bruised right knee, a sore right thumb, and a sprained left ankle—from a collision at second base three days earlier. The Indians were losing, 6-4, in the seventh inning, with the bases loaded, two outs, and Thurman Tucker, a left-handed batter, due to bat next. When Yankees manager Bucky Harris brought his ace southpaw reliever, Joe Page, into the game, Boudreau put himself in as a pinch hitter.

"When I stepped out of the dugout with a bat in my hands and field announcer Jack Cresson intoned, 'Attention please. Batting for Tucker, No. 5, Lou Boudreau,' the fans went crazy. Their cheers were deafening and sent a chill up my spine. I forgot about how badly my ankle hurt, or that my back was stiff, or that my thumb was so sore I could hardly grip the bat."

Boudreau slashed a single to center, driving in two runs to tie the score, and the Indians went on to win, 8-6. They also beat the Yankees in the nightcap, taking over first place and eventually winning the pennant and World Series.

At the time Boudreau put himself in to bat for Tucker, Indians owner Bill Veeck, seated in the press box, told one of the writers, "Even if Boudreau doesn't get a hit, this is the most courageous thing I've ever seen in baseball."

When Boudreau was inducted into the Baseball Hall of Fame in 1970, Bowie Kuhn, then-commissioner of baseball said in his introduction of the former shortstop-manager:

"The most remarkable thing about this remarkable man was the way he stretched the wonderful skills he had into superlative skills. As a shortstop, he was a human computer; he knew all the moves of the base runners, he knew what the pitcher was going to pitch. He had an instinct for where the ball would be hit, and from all of this he fashioned the wonderful ball player that we knew as Lou Boudreau.

"There are hitters in the Hall of Fame with higher life-time batting averages, but I do not believe there is in the Hall of Fame a baseball man who brought more use of intellect and avocation of mind to the game than Lou Boudreau."

Alva Bradley

(Owner, 1927-46)

Shortly after Alva Bradley and two partners bought the Indians on November 17, 1927, he wrote a letter to Ed Barrow, owner of the New York Yankees. It was a bid by Bradley to purchase from the Yankees a rookie first baseman who was holding out for more money.

Bradley's initial offer for the player, $150,000, was rejected, after which the owner of the Indians raised his bid to $175,000, plus Indians first baseman George Burns, and subsequently to $250,000, but Barrow still said no.

The rookie first baseman was Lou Gehrig, who was elected to the Hall of Fame in 1939.

When Roger Peckinpaugh was fired as the Indians manager after the 1941 season, Bradley disclaimed any responsibility with the statement: "I hire the manager, but the fans fire him."

And of his decision to appoint Lou Boudreau as the team's player-manager, replacing Peckinpaugh, Bradley said, "The more I inspected the qualifications of various other candidates, the more I became convinced that we couldn't afford not to take advantage of (Boudreau's) natural gift of leadership.

"I didn't know of another man of whom I could be so certain that he would be thoroughly respected by the players, press, and public. Lou is smart, he's a great ballplayer, a fine young man, a fighter, and a leader," Bradley said upon introducing Boudreau as the new manager of the Indians on November 25, 1941.

Larry Brown

(Shortstop/second baseman, 1963-71)

"We had started the 1966 season with 10 straight victories and won 13 of our first 14 games—though we still were only one game ahead of Baltimore—when we went into New York (May 4) for a series against the Yankees. Bob Friend pitched the opener for the Yankees, and I was playing shortstop, although, in all honesty, I don't remember playing the game. What I'm telling you is what people told me later.

"(Left fielder) Leon Wagner and I collided under a pop fly that Roger Maris hit in the fourth or fifth inning. The ball was headed for the left-field corner of Yankee Stadium, where the distance is about 300 feet (from the plate), but the wind was blowing from left to center and brought the ball back. I went out and Wags came in, and we ran together and hit head on. I don't know if he yelled or if I yelled. As I said, I really don't remember much about the whole thing.

"Anyway, you know what people say, that all men are created equal? Well, I can tell you they're not. (In the collision) Wags took the skin off his nose, that's all, and I almost died, right there on the field. My skull was fractured above both eyes; I had two broken cheekbones, a broken nose, and was hemorrhaging from every cavity in my head. I was out, unconscious for something like three days.

"When my wife came to New York and went to the hospital, they told her I was in the intensive care unit. She went in but couldn't find me. She told the nurse, 'My husband's not here,' and the nurse said, 'Yes, he is. That's him over there.' I was such a mess she didn't recognize me. It was a pretty ugly thing, for her as well as me.

"I finally woke up after three days, and you know, with a bad head injury, you don't know what you're doing. One thing I do remember is that I kept hearing this beep, beep, beep, and it was really bothering me. I said to the nurse, 'What's that noise, that beeping noise?' and she told me it was a heart monitor for the man in the bed next to me. I said, 'Well, turn it off, it's bothering me,' and she said, 'We can't turn it off. If we do, he'll die.' And I said, 'I don't care. The noise is killing me.' That's how bad I was.

"I was in the hospital 18 days and didn't play again for six weeks, exactly 43 days after the collision. You know, when you're fighting for your job every year as I was, you want to get back out there as fast as you can, although I shouldn't have played as soon as I did. They flew me back to Cleveland for surgery, and I had lost about 10 pounds, lying around the hospital.

"When I did get back (in the lineup), ironically the first game I played was in Yankee Stadium where the collision had taken place. When I was introduced in the starting lineup, I got a standing ovation from the fans, right there in Yankee Stadium. It was really neat . . . probably was the only one I ever got.

"Don't try to tell me the fans in New York are all bad."

Ernie Camacho

(Pitcher, 1983-87)

As an Indians reliever from 1983-87, Ernie Camacho enjoyed two splendid seasons as one of the American League's best closers in 1984 and 1986, when he was credited with 23 and 20 saves, respectively.

He also is "credited" with some verbal gems by the three beat writers who covered the Tribe during Camacho's tenure—Paul Hoynes of the *Cleveland Plain Dealer*, Jim

Ingraham of the *Lake County News-Herald*, and Sheldon Ocker of the *Akron Beacon-Journal*.

According to the three scribes, the best of Camacho's malapropisms were:

"What states are Massachusetts and Oklahoma City in?" and "Were there any black catchers in the Negro leagues?"

And after he blew a crucial save during the 1987 season, Camacho explained, "My arm was tired because before the game I had to sign 100 baseballs at one time, while the other guys on the team signed them over three days."

Tom Candiotti

(Pitcher, 1986-91)

"In 1986, when we were playing the Seattle Mariners in the last game of the season, I was all packed up and ready to go home because I'd pitched two days previously. At the time I was tied with Bert Blyleven (who then pitched for Minnesota) with 16 complete games, and I figured I'd just spend the day in the dugout watching the game, and leave as soon as it was over.

"But when I got to the clubhouse (manager) Pat Corrales came up to me and said, 'You're pitching today, and you're going to finish the game, no matter what.'

"Pat wanted to make sure that I wound up with the complete-game championship—one of the few things we (Indians) won that season—and we beat the Mariners, 4-2. But it wouldn't have mattered if I'd given up 14 or 15 runs, he would have left me out there.

"Blyleven had pitched for us (from 1981) until he was traded (August 1, 1985) to the Twins, which I think was Corrales' motivation for making sure that I finished ahead of Bert in complete games."

Rico Carty

(First baseman/designated hitter, 1974-77)

It was a stunning acceptance speech delivered by Rico Carty upon his introduction at a banquet attended by 600 fans honoring him as the Indians "Man of the Year" for 1976.

With Manager Frank Robinson seated next to him at the head table, Carty criticized Robinson for a lack of leadership.

"They talk about the leader of the team. They mention this player and that player. But who is the best leader of the team? It's the manager. When he leads, we got a ball club. Believe me, I'm telling this with all my heart," said Carty, as Robinson winced. So did General Manager Phil Seghi, seated next to Robinson, and virtually all the players among the audience.

Carty ended his remarks by saying to Robinson, "We need your help, Frank. If you don't help us, we'll all be in trouble."

Two months later, on June 7, 1977, Carty was suspended by Robinson for 15 days for "insubordination."

And before Carty's suspension was lifted, Robinson was fired (June 19).

Joe Charboneau

(Outfielder, 1980-82)

"It happened in 1980 and was the biggest thrill of my baseball career. We were in Yankee Stadium, and just being there was very exciting. Before the game, I went out to see the monuments in center field and I talked to Reggie Jackson (then a Yankee outfielder). Somebody took a picture of us, which I still have hanging on my wall at home.

"Tom Underwood, a left hander, was pitching for the Yankees, and the first time I faced him I got ahead in the count, 3-and-1, and looked for a fastball in, which I got. I swung, and it was the best I ever hit a ball. It ended up in the third deck, and after the game they told me it was one of the three longest balls ever hit in Yankee Stadium. Imagine that! Yankee Stadium. The 'House that Ruth built.'

"I remember going around second base, and the crowd was totally silent. I looked up to where the ball landed and thought to myself that I'd never hit another ball like that one—and I never did. It was a once-in-a-lifetime swing. A perfect swing, and the pitch was right there. The whole thing was unbelievable. It seemed like the ball carried forever— which the memory of it does."

Allie Clark

(Outfielder/first baseman, 1948-51)

Indians owner Bill Veeck and vice president Hank Greenberg were astonished—and, according to sources, infuriated—when player-manager Lou Boudreau assigned outfielder Allie Clark to play first base in the one-game playoff against the Boston Red Sox for the pennant in 1948.

The move also surprised Clark, who'd never previously played the position.

"I still don't have any idea why Boudreau decided to play me at first base, other than to get my (right-handed) bat in the lineup. After we'd lost that last game of the season (to Detroit, 7-1, in Cleveland), we showered, got dressed, went to the station, and rode the train all night to Boston.

"Lou never said anything to me, and when I got to the clubhouse (at Fenway Park) there was a first baseman's glove in my locker. I don't know whose it was. Maybe it was Boudreau's, because he could play any position. I took it and went into Boudreau's office and asked him, 'Lou, is this right?' He said, 'Yeah, you're playing first base.' That's all. So I did.

"Sure, I was scared. I'd never played first base before and remember, the Red Sox had a guy named Ted Williams and a couple other pretty good left-handed hitters in their lineup. I didn't know anything about playing first base.

"I was the happiest guy in the world when Boudreau took me out and put in Eddie Robinson (after the Indians had taken a 5-1 lead in the fourth inning). Actually, I guess I did OK. I went 0-for-2, but I fielded one grounder and took four throws without doing anything wrong.

"The amazing thing about it, if I had done something to lose the game, I wouldn't have been blamed. You know who would have taken the heat? Boudreau. That's the kind of manager he was. He'd play his hunches; he'd do anything he thought would help win a game. I thought he was a helluva manager and especially a helluva player."

Rocky Colavito

(Outfielder, 1955-59, 65-67)

On June 10, 1959, Rocky Colavito became the sixth player in major league history to hit four home runs in one game in the modern era (since 1901), and the third American Leaguer to do so. Since then, four players (all National Leaguers) have hit four, though only Colavito, Lou Gehrig in 1932, and Mike Schmidt in 1976 hit four in consecutive trips to the plate.

"My son Stevie remembers the night I did it (in Baltimore) better than anyone," said Colavito. "Every anniversary of that game he gets another picture of me made and framed that says, 'Happy 42nd,' or whatever year it is, which I think is a beautiful thing.

"Funny thing that night, early in the game, after I'd hit my first home run and as I caught a ball against the right-field wall, a guy in the stands threw a cup of beer in my face. I was livid and challenged him. I didn't think anybody should do something like that to a player who was trying to make a living.

"The next time up I hit my second home run, and when I got out to right field I told him that I'd meet him outside the stadium after the game.

Rocky Colavito

"So then, when I hit my third home run, the fans in right field gave me a standing ovation and guess what? The guy who threw the beer in my face was one of them. He was standing there cheering with the rest of the fans.

"But after I hit the fourth home run, he was gone.

"Something else that's funny about that night. Before the game I was asked by a sportswriter, 'When are you going to start hitting?' He was being facetious, but I knew that he also was partly serious. I was only 3-for-28 going into that game. "I told him, 'You never know, maybe I'll get going tonight.' Which I did.

"I remember everything about that game. I walked my first time at-bat—Jerry Walker was the Baltimore starting pitcher—and I hit my first homer off him with a man on base in the third inning. The ball hugged the left-field foul line, and while I knew it was long enough, there was a question of whether it was high enough.

"Nobody was on base when I hit the second homer in the fifth off Arnold Portocarrero. It was the best of the four, and went deep into the (left-field) stands far from the foul line.

"I hit No. 3, also off Portocarrero, in the sixth with one man on. Both of them (off Portocarrero) were on good pitches, sliders that hit the outside part of the plate. I was able to reach over and get them.

"Before I went to the plate the fourth time in the ninth inning, my roomie, Herb Score, said to me, 'Go up there and hit the fourth one.' I remember telling him I'd be happy to get a single, and he said, 'Bull. Go up there and do it.'

"Ernie Johnson (the Orioles' ace reliever) was on the mound by then, and his first pitch was high and inside. I just raised my chin and the ball went under it. He probably thought I'd be looking away for the next pitch, so he came back up and in with another fastball. I was looking for it and connected. It also wound up in the left-field stands, and we won, 11-8.

"I was thrilled. I was aware that Gehrig was the only other player to hit four in a row, because he was my brother Vito's favorite player. Mine, too, until Joe DiMaggio came along. The crowd (15,883) gave me a standing ovation."

Pat Corrales

(Manager, 1983-87)

"Gabe Paul was getting up in his years (73) when I came in to manage the Indians (in 1983). Dave Garcia, who'd managed the team before I got to Cleveland, warned me that sometimes Gabe had trouble staying awake.

"Dave told me he used to put a paperback book in his pocket and would read it as soon as Gabe dozed off. He said he got in a lot of reading that way.

"But I came up with a different strategy, because I didn't want to waste that much time. As soon as Gabe dropped off, I would slap his desk and say, 'Gotta go now, Gabe.' He'd wake up and, not realizing how long he'd slept, he'd be too embarrassed to ask me to stay any longer."

Alvin Dark

(Manager, 1968-71)

"My first year in the big leagues was 1948 (as a short-stop for the Boston Braves), and the way we won the pennant, how easy it was, I thought, 'Man, we are going to play in the World Series every year.' I never realized until later how tough it was and what a big thing it is to win the pennant and get to the World Series.

"I found out in a hurry. When we lost to Cleveland and their great pitching staff, that's when I knew how really tough it is.

"We were lucky to win the first game of the Series, and probably wouldn't have if it hadn't been for (umpire) Bill Stewart's call (in the eighth inning when Bob Feller tried to pick off pinch runner Phil Masi at second base). Stewart was a great (N.L.) umpire, but he called that play wrong, and everybody in the ballpark knew he blew it. Masi was out, or should have been called out.

"We knew the Indians had the play and that Feller and (shortstop Lou) Boudreau worked it good, but it just so happened that . . . uh, well, Masi was out.

"I was kneeling in the on-deck circle, because I was up next (following Tommy Holmes) and naturally, as soon as Feller turned (to throw to Boudreau) I stood up to see the play. When Stewart called Masi safe, I almost clapped my hands. I'm standing there thinking, 'Man, he was out, how in the world did the umpire call him safe?'

"Then Holmes singled to score Masi and we won, 1-0. But the man was out and everybody in our dugout—heck, everybody in Braves Field—knew it. I believe Stewart knew it too, that after he called it, he knew he called it wrong.

"But then, as Feller once told me, if Stewart had called Masi out, it's still a 0-0 game, and we might still be playing."

"When I managed the Indians (1968-71) all kinds of things were happening with Sam McDowell, who was one of my favorite guys and should have been a great, great pitcher. I loved Sam McDowell, I really did, but he was his own worst enemy.

"One time, when we were on a road trip in California, I was checking up on some of the players. Not all of them, but some of them, because I liked to have them in their rooms at a decent hour and it already was past the curfew. That's when I saw Sam walking down the hall in his undershorts.

"When he saw me he took off running out the back door of the hotel, jumped in the swimming pool and clung real close to the edge of the pool (in the water). He didn't think I could see him, and he just stayed there, hiding until I left. I was dying laughing, but I wouldn't do anything because if I did I'd get Jack Sanford, my pitching coach, mad at me."

Bob DiBiasio

(Vice President/Public Relations, 1979-86, 87-)

"The press box at the old Stadium was remodeled in the late 1970s and one of the features—as then Indians President Gabe Paul liked to point out—was that shatterproof and unbreakable glass panels were installed to protect the working media.

"However, one night in 1979 when we were playing California (Angels second baseman). Bobby Grich fouled off a pitch that flew up and hit one of the supposedly unbreakable glass panels in front of Dick Svoboda, who was covering for *United Press International.*

"Well, the unbreakable glass broke, the ball went right through the panel, and hit Svoboda in the head, which in itself was bad enough.

"But then to make matters worse, a couple of pitches later, after Svoboda changed his seat, Grich fouled off another one that hit the panel in front of Svoboda's new seat, and it also broke the glass.

"Except for a couple of scratches and bruises, Svoboda was OK, although his pride was seriously shattered, along with the window panels.

"So much for the unbreakable glass windows at the old Stadium."

Larry Doby

(Outfielder, 1947-55, 58)

"Winning the World Series was the highlight of my career, and I'll always cherish the memory of Steve Gromek hugging me. It was completely, totally spontaneous; we just grabbed each other because we were so happy to win (Game 4, 2-1, when Doby hit a home run and Gromek scattered seven hits to beat the Boston Braves and Johnny Sain).

Larry Doby

"As they say, God works in mysterious ways. Here was a white guy and an African-American guy who are put together and win a game, and when it's over they don't wonder, 'Should I not do this because I'm white and he's black? Or because 'I'm black and he's white?'

"No, they just do it, they just hug each other because they're happy, which made up for everything I went through. I would always relate back to that whenever I was insulted or rejected by hotels. I'd always think back to that picture of Gromek and me. It would take away all the negatives."

"I roomed with Satchel Paige, but I can't say we were close. It wasn't so much that Satch was a loner. It was how he dealt with people, those he knew, and he knew an awful lot of people because he'd pitched in all the towns that we played in.

"He'd been in those towns long, long ago. Not just like two or three years . . . it was more like 10 or 12 years previously. So all the black hotels that we lived in, he knew all the people, he was comfortable with them.

"Another reason I wasn't really close to Satch, I abided by the rules, and he didn't. Not always. You can't have different rules for different people. Everybody has to go by the same rules. Everybody has the same curfew, or should. That's the way it is, or should be."

Al Rosen, who was Doby's teammate from 1947-55, said of the former outfielder: "This is not to denigrate Jackie Robinson, but Jackie was a college educated man who had been an officer in the service and who played at the Triple-A level. Jackie was brought in by Branch Rickey specifically to be the first black player in major league baseball.

"Larry Doby came up as a second baseman who didn't have time to get his full college education, and who was forced to play a different position in his first major league season. I think, because of those circumstances, he had a more difficult time than Jackie Robinson. I don't think he has gotten the credit he deserves.

"I saw Larry get knocked down on four straight pitches by Dizzy Trout (of the Detroit Tigers), but Larry just got up, brushed himself off and walked to first base. I've always admired him."

Larry Dolan

(Owner, 2000-)

Upon purchasing the Indians on November 4, ~~1990~~ 2000, Larry Dolan said: "Dick (Jacobs) is my greatest asset and my greatest liability. He's an asset because of all the outstanding things he's done for this organization and this city. But he's a liability, because he's going to be a tough act to follow."

And, "My idol was always Lou Boudreau. It never occurred to me to be Bill Veeck."

Frank Duffy

(Shortstop, 1972-77)

"I liked being an Indian, and I really enjoyed my time in Cleveland (1972-77), even though the old Stadium was a tough ball park to play in. I think my (batting) average was better on the road than at home, one of the reasons being that Gaylord (Perry) loved long grass in the infield so that ground balls he threw didn't get through. But I hit a lot of ground balls, and a lot of mine didn't get through, either. So, statistically, offensively the Stadium hurt me, and it was cold, like a big cavern sometimes.

"But, talking about the whole thing, living in Cleveland and playing for Frank (Robinson) was my best time in baseball. One of my favorite memories, maybe the best of all, was the Opening Day game in 1975 when Frank hit a home run (off the New York Yankees' Doc Medich). What a way to start (his career) as major league baseball's first black manager!

"I wasn't in the lineup that day because I'd pulled a rib cage muscle in the last spring training game and missed the first 10 or 12 games. I was in the dugout and remember what it was like when Frank came around the bases. There were about 75,000 fans in the Stadium that day, and 7,500 the next day. That's how it always was in April in Cleveland, with the weather and school still going on.

"I thought playing for Frank was great, though some of the guys on that club had a little problem with him. I don't think it was ever racially motivated, at least not that I knew of. It's just that Frank came in and was still more like a player than a manager. He was still too close to being only a player. Everything came so easy for him as a player, unlike the way it was for most of the rest of us."

"Being traded to Cleveland (November 29, 1971) was a big break for me. I'd been at Cincinnati (1970-71), where I didn't play much because they had Dave Concepcion. Then I got traded to the Giants where Chris Speier was the shortstop, and I was just basically sitting. We had a young club in Cleveland, with a lot of good talent coming up—Jack Brohamer and Buddy Bell and Rick Manning and Dennis Eckersley—and we were really a team of equals, socially speaking.

"It was different when I was traded to Boston (March 24, 1978) where everything was stratified. The Red Sox had their superstars—Yaz (Carl Yastrzemski) and Jim Rice and Fred Lynn—a bunch of middle-echelon players, and then the bench guys, of which I was one, and it wasn't much fun.

"I wasn't really shocked when the Indians traded me, because I could see the handwriting, but I was disappointed, really disappointed. (General manager) Phil Seghi called me into his office and said, 'Hey, you should be happy. You're going to a strong club,' which the Red Sox were. But I knew I wasn't going to play much. Rick Burleson was their shortstop, and I didn't want to be a utility player, which I was all of 1978 and part of 1979, before I was released in the second year of a two-year contract. That was it for me, so I just said goodbye and made the transition."

Dennis Eckersley

(Pitcher, 1975-77)

"It was the most humbling experience of my career (1975-98) and happened as we were being introduced on Opening Day in 1976. I was really pumped and went charging out of the dugout onto the field at the old Stadium. But I missed the top step and took a headlong dive, flat on my face. It was terrible, humiliating, because in those days in Cleveland, the opener usually was the only time that everybody got jazzed up for the Indians and the stands were packed (with 58,478 fans).

"Fortunately, I didn't hurt myself—physically, that is—although my ego was shattered. Really shattered. Nobody said anything, because I think they were as embarrassed as I was."

A year later, on May 30, 1977, Eckersley pitched a no-hitter, beating California, 1-0, at the Stadium, fully restoring his shattered ego.

"(In that game against the Angels) I remember being on the mound in the ninth inning, all fired up, and then noticing that Jim Kern and Dave LaRoche were throwing bullets in the bull pen. I was thinking, 'Here I am, pitching my ass off, and they've got two guys throwing fire in the bull pen. I've got a no-hitter going, and if I give up a hit, I'm probably gone.' Of course, it was a 1-0 game . . . we scored in the first inning, but got nothing after that against Frank Tanana.

"Something else I recall is that I was yelling at Tanana most of the game. I guess I was doing it because (manager) Frank Robinson didn't like Tanana, for whatever reason. I did whatever made Robbie happy, and whatever he did. If he yelled at somebody, I did, too.

"But nobody in our dugout said (bleep) to me. They all stayed away from me. Every inning, same thing. It was like a ritual.

"When I got the second out in the ninth, I looked over to Buddy (Bell) at third base and yelled, 'One more out!' I was pretty cocky then, but Buddy didn't say anything. I think he was too nervous, because the pressure is on the fielders as much as the pitcher. Nobody wants to screw it up.

"In those days I was young and stupid to think that I could throw a no-hitter every time I pitched. And then, every time I'd give up my first hit I'd curse to myself and get mad, which sounds kind of crazy, I know, but that's how I felt back then."

Doc Edwards

(Catcher, 1962-63; Coach, 1985-87;
Manager, 1987-89)

"One day in 1986, when Pat Corrales was the manager (1984-87) and I was a coach, we were playing Baltimore at the Stadium. I was in our bullpen in left field and noticed something that (Orioles shortstop) Cal Ripken was doing. He was relaying the catcher's signals to the outfielders so they'd know what pitch was coming. Ripken put his right (bare) hand behind his back before every pitch and, when the catcher called for a curve ball he'd close his fist, or leave it open for a fast ball.

"We arranged for me to relay the information to our guy who was on deck (to bat next) and he would yell something to the batter to let him know what pitch to expect. The way we'd do it, I'd lean against the fence in front of the bullpen with my right arm up if it was a fast ball, and drop my hand to my hip if it was a breaking ball.

"We scored ten runs—ten runs!—that game, but here's how bad we were: we still lost, 11-10, because we had so many pitching problems. We had them all year.

"Ripken is a pretty smart guy, and the next day he stopped using his hand signals, probably because he either figured out what was happening—or maybe one of our players leaked to him what we were doing, though I hate to think any of our guys would do something like that.

"Stealing the other team's signals is all part of the game. Like (Bob) Feller always said, 'All's fair in love and war—and in baseball, when you're trying to win a pennant.' "

"When I played in Cleveland (1962-63) I roomed with Sam McDowell, who was only 19 or 20 then and was as pure as the driven snow. Duke Sims and Joe Azcue also caught Sam, and we all agreed on one thing, that McDowell had the four greatest pitches of any one man in the history of the game. I don't know of any pitcher who could throw all four pitches—fast ball, curve ball, slider and change-up—as good as McDowell.

"After I left the Indians and then got traded to the Yankees from Kansas City, we were in a ball game against Cleveland, and Sam had punched (struck) me out three times in a row. The fourth time I batted against him, in the bottom of the ninth, there were two outs and we were losing, 1-0. I was behind in the count, 0-and-2, and I knew I couldn't hit his fastball, or curve or slider. I knew if he threw me one of those three pitches, I'd go down for the fourth time, and the game would be over.

"But instead of a fast ball, curve, or slider, Sam threw me a change up, and I hit a dying quail over second base. You've seen on TV, when birds get shot and they just kind of flutter down to the ground. That's the way my ball looked when I hit Sam's change up. Don't ask me why he threw me a change-up. Probably just to fool me, have some fun at my expense.

"So now, instead of the game being over, I was on first and Elston Howard pinch hit for the pitcher. He swung late at one of Sam's fast balls and hit it into the right field seats to win the game.

"But the reason we won wasn't because Howard hit the home run, it was because McDowell threw me a change up instead of a fast ball, curve, or slider. I never said anything to him about it, because I was afraid I'd make him mad and, next time I'd bat against him, he'd hit me in the neck with a 110 mph fast ball."

John Efta

(Umpires room attendant, Jacobs Field, 1994-)

"Richie Garcia was umpiring at first base in a game one night in 1995 or 1996, and it happened to be his birthday. So, before the game started I told (then Indians manager) Mike Hargrove that if he got the opportunity it would be a nice gesture if he'd wish Garcia a happy birthday.

"Mike forgot about it when he went to the plate to turn in the lineup cards before the game, but as luck would have it, early in the game there was a close play at first base where Garcia was umpiring. Grover went out to argue and they're going nose-to-nose, hot and heavy, and finally Richie threw Hargrove out of the game.

"Grover kicked the ground and started to leave, but then he remembered what I'd told him, so he turned back and said to Garcia, 'Oh, by the way, Happy f———— Birthday.'

"And when the game was over I took Grover a piece of Garcia's birthday cake, and he loved it."

Harry Eisenstat

(Pitcher, 1939-42)

"As long as people talk about Bob Feller's career, how it started and how great he was, fans should remember me. I'm the guy who was the winning pitcher in 1938 (October 2) when Feller set the major league record (since broken) by striking out 18 batters in one game."

Eisenstat, who was with the Indians from 1939-42, pitched for Detroit in that 1938 game against Feller and had a no-hitter going until the eighth inning. He wound up with a four-hitter and a complete game, 4-1, victory, though Feller got all the accolades because he struck out 18 batters.

Harry Eisenstat

"Only one time in my major league career (1935-42) did I ever intentionally try to hit a batter, and I was under orders (by Detroit catcher-manager Mickey Cochrane) to do so.

"It was in 1938, right after Hitler had come to power in Germany. I was pitching against Chicago and heard a bench jockey yelling from the White Sox dugout, 'Hey, Eisenstat. Hitler is looking for you and Greenberg.' At that time there were not many Jewish players in the major leagues.

"Cochrane also heard what the guy was yelling and came out to the mound. He told me, 'When that sonofabitch comes to the plate, if you don't hit him right between the eyes with your first pitch, you'll be on a bus to Toledo (and the minor leagues) tomorrow.

"And if he starts to come out after you, I'll toss you the ball, and you hit him with it again.'

"So I did. I threw at him and he ducked, but the ball hit the peak of his cap. When he got to first base I saw Greenberg (then the Tigers first baseman) talking to the guy and pounding his finger on his chest. The minute the game ended Greenberg ran into the White Sox clubhouse, chasing the guy who'd been yelling at me, and had to be restrained by (Chicago manager) Jimmy Dykes, otherwise he'd have killed him."

"When I was with the Indians in 1940 and we were having all that trouble with the manager (Oscar Vitt), we were in Detroit, fighting for the pennant late in the season, trying to hold on to first place. We'd just lost a tough game to the Tigers, and that night in the Booke-Cadillac Hotel— my room was on the 21st or 22nd floor—and my roommate (pitcher) Bill Zuber and I, left the window open because it was very warm and there was no air conditioning in those days.

"I had to get up during the night to go to the bathroom and while I was there, Zuber woke up and noticed that I wasn't in bed, and that the window was wide open. He started yelling, 'Eisie, Eisie,' and ran to the open window thinking I'd jumped because I was depressed that we had lost the game that day.

"When I heard him yelling, I ran out of the bathroom and saw him at the open window, and then I thought *he* was going to jump, so I started yelling, 'No, no, Bill, don't do it, it's not worth it.'

"He'd just put a deposit on a farm and was planning to pay it off with our World Series checks, and all he could think about was, there goes the farm. When he saw me, he said, 'Why the hell didn't you tell me you were going to the bathroom?'

"I said to him, 'What do you want me to do, wake you up every time I take a leak?'"

In 1937, when he pitched for Detroit, Eisenstat was the winning (relief) pitcher in both games of a double header, in which future Hall of Famer Hank Greenberg hit three home runs to provide all the offensive support the Tigers needed. "After the games," said Eisenstat, "(manager) Mickey Cochrane told everybody, 'Fellas, lock yourselves in your rooms tonight. The Jews in Detroit will be going crazy.'"

"Once, when Greenberg and I went to the synagogue for Yom Kippur, the congregation saw Hank and started to applaud. The rabbi didn't know why . . . he thought they were clapping for him."

Ed Farmer

(Pitcher, 1971-73)

"We were going to be on the 'Game of the Week,' one time in 1972, and Curt Gowdy, who did the game on television, came to our early workout. Gowdy was a good friend of Warren Spahn, our pitching coach, who was throwing batting practice. In those days pitchers hit for themselves, and I took (hit) one of Spahnie's pitches to the upper deck at the old Stadium. Gowdy saw it and yelled, 'Spahnie, I never saw anyone hit a pitch from you that far.'

"Well, anyone who knows Spahnie knows how competitive he is, and when Gowdy said what he did, that was the end of batting practice. Spahn started throwing curve balls, sinkers, screwballs, and change-ups, and even though he was then in his 50s, the old guy could still pitch.

"I said to him, 'What the hell is this?' and he said, 'Sometimes batting practice becomes pitching practice,' which it was for him—and all because Gowdy got on him for the ball I hit.

"I said to Spahnie, 'You retired 20 years ago, can we hit now?' and he said no, which was the end of it—but not until after he threw a fastball behind me."

"One of the first things I learned in the big leagues was in a game against the Giants when I was pitching to Willie McCovey. I threw a pitch that was about two inches —at least—wide of the plate and Ed Runge, who was umpiring, called it a strike.

"McCovey turned around and said something to Runge, and my next pitch was three or four inches wide, but Runge called it strike two. Now McCovey started raving and ranting, and when he went back to the bat rack to get some pine tar, (catcher) Ray Fosse came out to the mound and said, 'Runge just told me, throw it anywhere in the ball park, it'll be strike three, no matter where it is.'

"I asked Ray, 'Does he do that a lot?' and Ray said, 'No, just in certain instances.' And when my next pitch wasn't even close, Runge called it strike three. McCovey just shook his head and walked away. I think he learned a lesson. I know I did."

Bob Feller

(Pitcher, 1936-41, 45-56)

During the 1948 season, when the Indians fought the Boston Red Sox and two other teams (New York and Philadelphia) for the pennant, a high-powered telescope from Bob Feller's World War II ship, the U.S.S. Alabama, was hidden in the center field scoreboard at the old Cleveland Municipal Stadium. It was used to steal opposing catchers' signals.

"All's fair in love and war—and in baseball, when you're trying to win a pennant," Feller said. "The way I felt about it, it was like in the war, you had to decipher a code, break it down, which we did against the Germans and the Japanese, and we won (World War II), right?"

And the Indians won the 1948 American League pennant and World Series.

Bob Feller

Feller struggled through most of the 1948 season, finishing with a sub-par (for him) 19-15 won-lost record. It resulted in speculation that his career as one of baseball's greatest pitchers was near the end, to which he quipped: "I must've been the cleanest guy in the game because the writers kept saying I was all washed up."

"The 1948 season was not one of my best, though it certainly was for the Indians. We had a bunch of great guys, and some pretty tough guys, too. Al Rosen, who came up late in the season, was one of them. A real tough guy.

"After we won the playoff game (for the pennant), Rosen, Joe Gordon, and a couple other teammates and I were sitting at the bar in the Kenmore Hotel. Two guys who looked like lumberjacks came along and started harassing us, especially Rosen. One of them tapped Al on the shoulder and said, 'Hey, Rosen, what are you doing here?' Rosen asked him, 'What do you mean, what am I doing here?'

"The guy was very offensive and abusive, and finally Rosen said, 'Tell me, are we bothering you?' And he said, 'No, you're not bothering me,' and Rosen said, 'Well, you're bothering the hell out of me' and hit him right on the button, knocked him on his butt. It was a terrible mess.

"The guy didn't know that Rosen had been the heavyweight boxing champion of Florida when he went to the University of Miami.

"If something like that happened today it'd be in all the papers, Al probably would get sued, the commissioner would come down on him, and it probably would cost him a nice piece of change. But things were different then."

"If it hadn't been for baseball, I probably would have spent my life picking corn in Iowa, and I've got my father to thank for that. He taught me how to play baseball instead of how to shoot a rifle—and to not cause trouble, which more fathers ought to do with their sons now."

Ray Fosse

(Catcher, 1967-72, 76-77)

"Catching Sam McDowell was something else. He had four of the greatest pitches of any pitcher I ever caught. He had a hellacious fast ball, a hard breaking curve, a quick slider and a real good change up—and he was consistent with all of them. But Sam was funny about some things. He liked to trick batters. Do the unexpected.

"One night Dick Tracewski (of Detroit) hit a game-winning home run off a change up. This was after Sam had told me before the game that he was going to get Tracewski out on four different pitches—fastball, curve, slider, change up. He did with the first three, but when he threw him the change up, Trixie hit it for a home run that won the game for the Tigers.

"(Manager) Alvin Dark was beside himself, he was so upset with Sam. And what Sam said after the game didn't help any. Sam explained that he threw Tracewski a change-up, because he knew that Tracewski couldn't hit his fastball, but he knew he could hit Sam's change up. Therefore, in

Sam's mind, Tracewski would be looking for a fastball and Sam thought he'd cross him up with a change up."

Tito Francona

(Outfielder/first baseman, 1959-64)

"I know a lot of guys had trouble with Frank Lane, but I didn't. The fact is, I kind of liked the guy. After I joined the Indians in 1959, in my first time at bat as a pinch hitter I got a single that drove in the game-winning run. Lane came down to the clubhouse and gave me a check for $250.

"A week later I got another key hit, and this time Lane gave me $500, which was pretty good because my salary was $10,000 for the season.

"At the end of the season, after I hit .363, Lane called me up to his office and gave me a contract for 1960 for $20,000, a $10,000 raise. I didn't waste any time signing, and went down to the clubhouse to pack up my stuff to go home for the winter. (Manager) Joe Gordon asked me how much of a raise I got, and I told him, '$10,000.'

"Joe didn't say anything except to tell me to not leave the clubhouse. He went over to the phone and made a call. I didn't know who he called, but when he got off the phone, he told me to go back upstairs, that Lane wanted to see me again. I did and Lane had another contract already made out for me. It was for $2,500 more, for a total of $22,500.

"So, no, I don't dislike Lane . . . and I liked Joe Gordon a helluva lot, too."

"My relationship with John McHale was not as good as it was with Frank Lane when McHale ran the Tigers and I was with Detroit (in 1958), before I was traded to Cleveland. The previous winter (1957-58) I tried to get a $1,000 raise, but McHale flat-out refused, wouldn't even consider it, so I had no choice but to sign for what he was offering.

"But I got even with him a few years later . . . well, several years later when my son Terry graduated from the University of Arizona.

"Terry had been a big star in college and was picked by Montreal in the first round of the (1980) amateur draft. McHale was then the general manager of the Expos, so when it came time for them to sign Terry, I told him, 'Let me do it (the negotiations), I know John McHale very well.' Boy, did I ever.

"A few days later McHale called with an offer, and Terry gave me the phone. Right off I asked McHale, 'Do you remember that $1,000 raise you wouldn't give me when we both were with Detroit?' McHale said he didn't remember, so I told him, 'Well I do, and if you want to sign my son, it's going to cost you a $300,000 signing bonus.'

"Terry was listening in the other room and almost fainted when he heard what I said. But it set the stage for a real good contract for Terry—a signing bonus of $100,000, which at that time was very good."

Vern Fuller

(Second baseman, 1964, 66-70)

"One night we were in the middle innings of a game and I looked in at the plate and saw Joe Azcue, who was catching, leaving the field and going into the dugout even though there were only two outs.

"Then I realized why. Joe forgot his mask. He caught for the first two batters without a mask! It was crazy. I said to Brownie (shortstop Larry Brown), 'Look, Joe wasn't wearing a mask.' Brownie laughed and said, 'With a puss like Joe's, it wouldn't matter if they fouled a pitch off his face or not.'

"After the inning Joe told us that he just forgot his mask, and nobody reminded him. Imagine that. Neither the umpire nor either of the two guys who batted asked him why he wasn't wearing his mask. Joe said, 'All of a sudden I realized I didn't have it on, so I just called time and went in and got it.'

"Then he said, 'But that was the only time I ever did that,' although, knowing Joe, I wouldn't bet on it."

Wayne Garland

(Pitcher, 1977-81)

As one of baseball's first free agents in the winter of 1975-76, Wayne Garland signed with the Indians for what was then the largest contract in the game—$2.3-million over 10 years. At the time, the minimum salary in the major leagues was $19,000, and the average salary the preceding season was $51,500.

"I was coming off a pretty good season, 20-7 with Baltimore, and my agent, Jerry Kapstein, was collecting offers," said Garland. The contract called for him to receive a $300,000 signing bonus, and he was guaranteed annual salaries of $200,000 through 1986. "Thirteen clubs wanted to sign me, and Los Angeles offered a five-year deal for something like $1.2 million, which is what we were basing our negotiations on. Basically, a million dollars.

"Then, one night Kapstein called and said, 'Wayne, I've got you a real good contract, though I didn't get you a million dollars.' I said, 'Jerry, I understand that (the Dodgers' offer) was just what we were looking at, that it was the high scale, so whatever you got, I'm sure you did a helluva job.' Then he said, 'Well, I got you over two million . . . a 10-year contract for $2.3 million—all of it guaranteed, no cut, no trade—from the Indians.'

"I almost dropped the phone. I said, 'No way,' and Kapstein said, 'Yes.' "

However, in his second season with the Indians, Garland suffered a rotator cuff injury and subsequently underwent surgery. He attempted several comebacks, but never was able to live up to expectations and eventually was released, during the winter of 1981-82, despite his guaranteed contract.

"Right after the strike (in 1981) ended and we went back to finish the season, we (the Indians) were in the backup game on Monday night television, and I was scheduled to pitch. But Gabe Paul called up (manager) Dave Garcia and told him not to start me. He said he didn't want me to pitch on national TV and maybe embarrass the club.

"Things got progressively worse after that. I had to be in the bullpen even though I couldn't pitch. If I went out and pitched two innings or nine, my arm felt dead for three or four days afterwards, but they still wanted me to go to the bullpen and pitch in relief.

"They told me they were paying me a lot of money and that I should start earning it. I told them there was nothing I could do, because my arm wouldn't come back. It's not like I went out and hurt myself on purpose. It seemed like everyone held a grudge against me, because I was making what was big money then.

"But I didn't ask for it . . . they offered it. And who wouldn't have taken it?"

Pedro Gonzalez

(Second baseman, 1965-67)

As a good fielding but light-hitting second baseman from 1965-67, Pedro Gonzalez was once called a "Smiling Volcano," for reasons that often became obvious.

Once, in 1966, the Smiling Volcano erupted when the box score in the *Plain Dealer* did not credit him with a hit. However, it was a mistake in the newspaper as the line after his name read "4-1-0-1," for four at-bats, one run scored, no hits, and one run batted in, but should have been "4-1-1-1."

Gonzalez confronted the official scorer and demanded to know why he was not credited with a hit. The scorer tried to tell Gonzalez, "It was a typographical error," to which the now (un) Smiling Volcano responded, "Error! Error! How could it be an error? (The fielder) never touched the ball!"

Joe Gordon

(Second baseman, 1947-50)

During the clubhouse meeting following the final regular-season game in 1948 when the Indians finished in a tie with Boston, Manager Lou Boudreau announced that Gene Bearden would pitch the playoff game against the Red Sox.

Several players were surprised, and some openly expressed their objection because Bearden would be taking the mound with only one day's rest. Johnny Berardino was the most vocal of the critics.

But second baseman Joe Gordon said, "Lou, we went along with your choice for 154 games and finished in a tie. There's not a man in this room who, two weeks ago, wouldn't have settled for a tie. I'm sure we can go along with you for another game."

And, after Boudreau hit two homers and Bearden pitched a five hitter to beat the Red Sox, 8-3, Gordon toasted his manager and double-play partner: "To the greatest leatherman I ever saw; to the damnedest clutch hitter that ever lived; to a doggone good manager, Lou."

In June of 1958, Frank Lane asked Gordon if he'd like to manage the Indians, Gordon replied, "Hell yes." Then

Lane asked when he could come to Cleveland to take over the team, Gordon said, "Yesterday." And what about (contract) terms? "The hell with terms," Gordon said, ending the "negotiations."

Johnny Goryl

(Coach, 1982-88)

"A lot of unusual things happened during my 50 years in professional baseball, and one I remember best was in 1986 (May 27) during a game at the old Stadium against Boston. The Red Sox had just gone ahead, 1-0, in the top of the sixth inning when fog started rolling in off the lake. Mike Brown was on the mound for the Red Sox, and Dwight Evans, the Red Sox right fielder, complained to the second base umpire that he couldn't see the hitter or the pitch to the plate because of the fog.

"So the umpires stopped the game and got Bobby Bonds, then one of our coaches, to hit fungoes—fly balls— to Evans in right field, to see if he really couldn't see the ball. We were sitting in the dugout and watched the balls go out there. We could see them pretty good, though Evans made like he couldn't. Naturally, he wanted the umpires to call the game, which they finally did, because the fog never lifted. And because five innings had been played, it counted as a regulation game, a victory for the Red Sox.

"It would have been very bad if that one loss had cost us the pennant, or even a higher place in the standings, though it didn't. We weren't very good and finished in fifth place.

"After the game was called off, Oil Can Boyd, a pitcher for the Red Sox, said in all seriousness, 'That's what they get for building this stadium next to the ocean,' which capped a crazy day."

Mudcat Grant

(Pitcher, 1958-64)

"Years back they used to use pitchers for pinch runners, and one time, early in the 1962 season, we were in Kansas City and Mel McGaha was the manager. That's smart Mel McGaha, and our first base coach was Ray Katt.

"We'd lost the front end of a double header and late in the second game (Jim) Piersall got a single and McGaha put me in to run. Piersall had a sore leg or something, and I was pretty fast then, and we needed the run. When I got to first base Katt told me, 'Mudcat, if this guy hits a 'tweener, I want you to run like you done stole two watermelons and the farmer is chasing you with a shotgun.'

"Well, I was pretty level then, but somehow what he said hit me wrong. I said, 'To hell with you,' which is making what I really said sound pretty good, and I walked off the field. Katt yelled, 'No, no, come back, come back,' but I wouldn't. He knew he was in trouble for what he'd said, but I wouldn't go back.

"I went across the infield (to the Indians dugout on the third base side) because, that way I knew it would hold up the game. When I got to our dugout McGaha said, 'Get your ass back out there,' and I said to him, 'To hell with

Mudcat Grant

you, too,' and finally they had to put somebody else in to run.

"Normally, when you're African-American and raised as a southern kid, you learn to handle comments like what Katt said. But back then, I was young and remember, it wasn't all that long after Jackie Robinson (broke the color barrier in baseball), so that's probably the reason I reacted the way I did."

"Another time, when we were in Cooperstown to play in the Hall of Fame game, Vic Power and I were on the field working out and we saw Ty Cobb in the other team's dugout. I said to Vic, 'That's Ty Cobb, let's go and shake his hand.'

"Well, even though we'd heard all those rumors that Cobb was a bad-ass racist, he was still Ty Cobb, and we wanted to shake his hand. So we went over and Vic said, 'Hi, Mr. Cobb. I'm Vic Power and this here is Mudcat Grant. He's a pitcher and I'm a first baseman and we want to shake your hand.'

Cobb looked at us and said, 'Hey, how you two nigger boys doin'? OK, I hope.'

"Well, me being from the south, and being just a boy, I thought, I don't care if he's Ty Cobb or who, but he's got a lot of nerve, though I didn't say anything.

"But Vic, who's Puerto Rican, went crazy. He said, 'You old somanabeech, how can you say something like that, you somanabeech.' I guess it kind of shook up Cobb because, next thing we know, we saw him kind of sneaking out of the ball park."

When Grant returned to Cleveland as one of the Indians' "100 Greatest Players," he was interviewed on the radio and told a few stories from his days as a pitcher for the Indians. The trouble was, a veteran sportswriter recognized several of the tales as not being totally factual, which didn't faze Mudcat one iota.

"Oh, that's what makes this so much fun," he said. "There ain't no fun telling a boring story."

Hank Greenberg

(Vice President/General Manager, 1948-57)

Hall of Fame outfielder/first baseman Hank Greenberg, who came to the Indians as farm director under Bill Veeck in 1948, then served as general manager from 1950-57, had a stormy relationship with the media in Cleveland.

It prompted Greenberg to remark, "The only way to get along with newspapermen is to be like Dizzy Dean. Say something one minute and something different the next."

Before his death in 1986, Greenberg was invited to return to Cleveland for a reunion of the 1954 team. He declined, saying, "The closest I ever want to get to Cleveland is 30,000 feet in the air, on my way somewhere else."

Alfredo Griffin

(Shortstop, 1976-78)

"When I played in Cleveland, I couldn't speak much English—I had trouble even ordering food in a restaurant—and Rico Carty was the one who helped me most. He was like a father to me, telling me how I was supposed to be on the field, and how to behave off the field. I liked him a lot.

"He also was a very funny guy, although not everybody saw that side of him. Once in 1979 when Rico and I were with the Blue Jays, Nolan Ryan, who was in his prime then, was going to pitch against us, and Ryan said in the paper that he was going to strike out 20 of us.

"Rico said, 'No he won't . . . maybe 17 or 18, but not 20,' which was pretty funny, because even if he didn't strike out 20, 17 or 18 were a lot. I don't know how many he did strike out, something like 14, but he won the game—and struck out Rico a couple of times, too.

"After Rico retired he wanted to become a politician in the Dominican Republic, but it didn't work. He didn't have the character to do that."

Steve Gromek

(Pitcher, 1941-53)

"After Gene Bearden pitched (and won) Game 3 of the 1948 World Series, giving us a 2-1 lead against the Boston Braves, Lou Boudreau called a team meeting and said that he'd decided to pitch me in the fourth game and save Bob Feller for the fifth.

"The way Boudreau explained it was, 'Instead of Feller, I'm willing to sacrifice and pitch Gromek, then come back with Feller.' The key word was 'sacrifice.' I didn't know what to think, although I knew it wasn't a compliment. What it did was motivate me, and I beat the Braves, 2-1, on Larry Doby's homer (off Johnny Sain) in front of the largest crowd (81,897) in baseball history at that time. It was the best game I'd pitched in a long time, so what Boudreau did was great for me and my career.

"A few years ago (in 1998 when the Indians celebrated the 50th anniversary of the 1948 team) I called Boudreau on the telephone and told him, 'I never thanked you for what you did, but I am thanking you now.' It turned out to be a big break for me. A lot of people remember me because of that game."

After Gromek's victory over the Braves in Game 4 of the World Series, he and outfielder Larry Doby, whose homer was the winning run, were photographed embracing in the Indians clubhouse. "I can talk about it now because the people involved are gone and times are different," recalled Gromek during the team's reunion in 1998.

Steve Gromek

"I'll never forget the reception I got from the pastor of my church when I returned home to Hamtramck (Michigan), after that picture of Doby and me appeared in the newspaper. I guess just about every newspaper in the country used the photo. The assistant pastor, who's also gone now, told me what happened.

"The two priests were having breakfast and reading about the game. When the pastor saw the picture of me hugging Larry, he said to the assistant pastor, 'Oh, my goodness, look at this. Steve is hugging a black man. How could he do something like that?'

"The assistant pastor said he looked at the photograph, read about Doby's game-winning home run, and replied, 'Father, if I were pitching in the World Series and a black guy hit a home run to win a game for me, I'd hug him, too.

"'In fact,' the assistant pastor said," according to Gromek, "'Father, if it had been me, I'd be so happy I wouldn't have just hugged him . . . I would've kissed his black ass.'

"Actually, I didn't kiss Larry, though I probably would have if the photographer had asked. What would be wrong about that? We had just won a big game and we both were as happy as could be."

Pedro Guerrero

(Minor league third baseman, 1977)

Though he never made it to the big leagues with the Indians, Pedro Guerrero was held in high esteem by the club before he was traded to the Los Angeles Dodgers for left-handed pitcher Bruce Ellingsen. Early in his career, Guerrero, who was born and raised in the Dominican Republic, had trouble mastering the English language. As he once said, "Sometimes sportswriters write what I say and not what I mean."

Sammy "Bad News" Hale

(Second baseman/third baseman, 1931, 33-40)

"I sure used my head on that one," Sammy Hale said after a game against Boston at Fenway Park on September 7, 1935. His comment was made after a line drive off the bat of Joe Cronin with the bases loaded tore through Hale's glove at third base. The ball ricocheted off Hale's forehead to shortstop Bill Knickerbocker, who caught it for one out, tossed to second baseman Roy Hughes for the second out, and Hughes' throw to first baseman Hal Trosky to complete what has to be one of the rarest triple plays in baseball history.

Mel Harder

(Pitcher, 1928-47; Coach, 1948-63

"In all the years I was in baseball—from 1928-47 as a pitcher for the Indians, and from 1948-69 as a pitching coach for the Indians, New York Mets, Chicago Cubs, Cin-

Mel Harder

cinnati Reds and Kansas City Royals—one of the funniest things I ever saw took place during a game at League Park in the early 1930s.

"Smead Jolley, who was a good hitter but not a real good outfielder, was playing right field for Chicago this particular day, and one of our guys hit a liner that Jolley backed up to catch, but the ball went right through his glove for an error (No. 1).

"Jolley turned around to play the ball off the wall, but it caromed off the concrete part, and before Jolley could get his glove down, it went through his legs for another error (No. 2).

"By now the batter was heading to second with Jolley chasing the ball as it rolled toward the infield, and by the time he got to it, our guy was going to third. Jolley picked up the ball and threw to third base, but it was wild and went into the stands for another error (No. 3), all on one play. I swear I never saw anything like it."

Harder was a member of the Indians in 1940 when they staged a rebellion against then-manager Oscar Vitt, which subsequently caused them to be called the "Cleveland Cry Babies."

"We had a good ball club—Bob Feller, Hal Trosky, Jeff Heath, Lou Boudreau, Ken Keltner and a lot more—and they all thought we had a good chance to win the pennant. But they didn't feel we could do it with Vitt managing," said Harder. "It was the way Vitt operated. He would pat you on the back one minute and criticize you behind your back the next. He was two-faced, and it finally got to some of the guys."

On June 13, 1940, they petitioned then-owner Alva Bradley to replace Vitt, though he refused to do so, and the

Indians lost the pennant to Detroit on the final weekend of the season. Nine days after the season ended, Bradley fired Vitt.

Mike Hargrove

(First baseman, 1979-85; Coach, 1990-91; Manager, 1991-99)

It was February 1999 and Mike Hargrove was starting his ninth season as manager of the Indians, who were seeking their fifth consecutive American League Central Division championship. On the first day of spring training Hargrove distributed tee shirts upon which the following message was printed, "Go hard or go home."

Eight months later Hargrove himself went "home," replaced as manager by Charlie Manuel, after the Indians won another division title but failed to reach the World Series.

Ken "The Hawk" Harrelson

(First baseman/outfielder, 1969-71)

Upon joining the Indians after being traded from the Red Sox in 1969, Ken Harrelson, who'd been a cult hero in Boston, was asked what kind of women he preferred. "Those that are breathing," he said.

John Hart

(Vice President/General Manager, 1991-2001)

"I'll never forget my first game as (interim) manager of the Indians. I had always aspired to manage in the major leagues, and spent my whole career in baseball until then working for that position. I finally did (become a major league manager) if only on an interim basis in 1989, late in the season, when I replaced Doc Edwards for the final month of the season.

"We were playing Detroit, and Bud Black was my starting pitcher against Frank Tanana. For six innings it's a nothing-nothing game, and I had Doug Jones sitting in the bullpen. When we went ahead, 1-0, in the seventh, I wanted to bring Jones in. Actually, I started asking Black in the sixth inning, and I kept asking him in the seventh and eighth how he was feeling, if he was getting tired. I really wanted to win, not only because it was my first game, it also was against a future Hall of Famer, Sparky Anderson, which made it even bigger to me.

"But Buddy kept telling me, 'John, I'll tell you when I get tired. Stop worrying. I'm feeling so good I want you to go and sit down at the end of the dugout and be quiet. I'm going to get you your first win. Just let me go back out there and don't worry about me.'

"So I didn't. I sat down at the end of the dugout and left him alone, and he got the Tigers out one-two-three in the ninth for my first win. I'll never forget it.

"It was something that only a few men have the opportunity to do . . . become a major league manager. Even though I was only an interim manager and I knew it would be for only a short time, it was very important to me, a guy who had fought through the minor leagues, managed all the way through them and finally had achieved a lifelong goal. I'd won my first game, and it was against a Hall of Famer. And so, yes, I was a little nervous. But Bud Black got it for me, just as he said he would—and we've been buddies ever since."

"Another time during a game I was managing, we were really struggling and had runners on first and second with nobody out. The batter was Joe Carter, whose statistics at the time were terrible . . . he was hitting under a hundred. I saw that the third baseman was playing all the way back, so I gave Joe the bunt sign, thinking we could surprise the third baseman.

"Well, what I did was surprise Joe. He stepped out of the batter's box and looked into the dugout at me with such a look on his face, I took off the bunt.

"But I shouldn't have . . . he hit into a double play."

Ron Hassey

(Catcher, 1978-84)

"Lenny Barker's perfect game was the second one I caught, which is something no other catcher has done. (Dennis Martinez threw the first, for Montreal, 2-0, against Los Angeles on July 28, 1991, and Barker, for the Indians, 3-0, against Toronto on May 15, 1981).

"Dennis and Lenny were both hard throwers, but with Dennis, I could tell around the fifth inning that something special could happen.

"With Lenny, although he had a good fast ball, when I realized that night what a good curve ball he also had, I kept calling for it. I think he shook me off only once and threw a change up that the batter popped up. After that he didn't shake me off the rest of the game.

"I like to recall both of those games, but to tell you the truth, I like to think more about Dennis's game. It makes me feel younger."

Von Hayes

(Outfielder, 1981-82)

"Before the Indians traded me (to the Philadelphia Phillies) in 1983, there were a lot of rumors that I'd be going somewhere, but I was still absolutely shocked when it actually happened.

"A lot of friends had been calling me up, teasing me by pretending they were Phil Seghi or Gabe Paul, and telling me I was traded. So, when the call did come from Seghi, I didn't believe him. I said, 'OK, who is this? I'm getting tired of this crap.' It took some doing for him to convince me it really was Seghi. He told me (the trade) was going to be good for me, that with Philadelphia I'd have an opportunity to play for a team that could win it right then and there. Which we (the Phillies) did.

"But, looking back on it, I kind of regret I didn't get the opportunity to stay with the Indians. Who knows? I might have been with Cleveland long enough to play in this beautiful ball park (Jacobs Field).

"I also wonder if my major league career would have lasted longer in Cleveland. My last season (1991 with the Phillies) I broke my arm when I was hit by a pitch from Tom Browning. And, yes, I think he was intentionally throwing at me, and I was finished. I tried to make a comeback with California (in 1992), but it was no good."

Jim Hegan

(Catcher, 1941-42, 46-57)

Though Jim Hegan's batting average never was anything to rave about, there's no doubt about the high esteem in which he was held by his peers as a catcher, as Birdie Tebbetts once said:

"You start and end any discussion of catchers with Jim Hegan. Add all the things a catcher has to do—catch, throw, call a game—and Jim Hegan was the best I ever saw."

Woodie Held

(Shortstop/second baseman/outfielder/ third baseman, 1958-64)

"Playing with Gary Bell and Tito Francona in Cleveland was like a comedy hour every day. Guys were laughing all the time. It was a fun clubhouse, although we didn't win too many games until 1959. That was a good year for us. We should have won the pennant.

"Gary, especially, kept everybody loose. He's one of the funniest men I've ever known. I used to tell him, the way you pitch, you should have been a comedian, though he knew I was only kidding. He was a very good pitcher. We were roommates for five years. I guess that's why we're both crazy, or at least why people think we're crazy.

"But (Bell) also has a temper. Especially the way he'd get mad at an umpire if he wasn't calling pitches the way Gary thought they should be called. When he'd get mad (manager) Joe Gordon used to tell me to go talk to Gary and calm him down. But just about every time I'd get to the mound Gary would say, 'What the hell are you doing here? Get your ass back to shortstop and leave me alone.' So I would. Like I said. He was a funny guy—most of the time."

"I was in Cleveland when Frank Lane traded managers, Gordon (to Detroit) for Jimmy Dykes (in 1960). Everybody on the team was shocked. We couldn't believe what he'd done, but that's the way Frank was. You never knew what to expect from him, which is the way he liked it. We also were shocked when he traded Rocky (Colavito) for Harvey Kuenn (in 1960), and a couple days later traded Herb Score for Barry Latman. I think Lane did a lot of that crazy stuff because he liked to see his name in the newspapers.

"Like most guys, I had trouble getting any money out of Lane. After I had a good year in 1959—I hit 29 home runs—he wanted to give me only a thousand dollar raise. Finally he went up to $2,000, and I told him I'd stay home before I'd play for what he was offering. Hell, 29 home runs for a shortstop was very good. I was OK in the field, too. I think I made 21 errors, but that wasn't bad. If you don't make any errors it means you never got to any balls.

"The way we wound up (contract negotiations), Lane agreed that if I was hitting .275 by the All-Star break, I'd get a brand new station wagon, which is what happened. I got a station wagon, which represented the raise I'd wanted, although I didn't get it in actual dollars."

"I was with the Yankees in Cleveland the night (May 7, 1957) that Gil McDougald's line drive hit Herb Score in the eye. I was in the bullpen and could hear the crack of the ball hitting Score all the way out there. It was awful. Poor Herb—but also, poor Gil. He was crying, couldn't stop crying, he felt so bad. Gil was the type of guy that things like that hurt him. He was very sensitive. I know a lot of guys think that (hitting Score with that line drive) hurt Gil's career. I don't know, maybe it did. As I said, he was very sensitive."

Orel Hershiser

(Pitcher, 1995-97)

"Cleveland, in 1995, was an unbelievable year, and while everybody tells you what happened on the field, let me tell you something that happened off the field.

"In the super (field) boxes around the (backstop) of the playing field they serve dessert to the high roller fans in the fourth or fifth inning. One day, during a game, I walked past the double doors that connect the dugout with those super boxes and saw the dessert cart between the crack in the doors, so I knocked.

"A girl came to the door and asked what I wanted. I told her I wanted some carrot cake. She gave me a piece and from then on, because I knew the dessert cart always came down there at the same time, between the fourth and fifth innings, I'd get dessert and go back behind the dugout and have coffee and cake—except when I was pitching.

"The manager (Mike Hargrove) never found out, and other guys probably are doing it now—and now it's going to be in your book and I'll be in trouble. So will the guys who are doing it since I left."

"That season (1995) was awesome. The biggest thing I remember about that team was how loose we were. I came from the Dodgers, a team that was a lot more professional— and by that I don't mean in a positive or negative way, where the Indians are concerned. That was the year of the bubble-gum bubbles on caps, and the hot foots and things like that. Wayne Kirby and (Alvaro) Espinoza were doing all kinds of pranks to keep people loose in the dugout and in the club-house.

"We had great players, and it's too bad we didn't win the World Series after getting so close (losing in six games). I lost the opener to Greg Maddux when I let the team down by walking two hitters in a row, Fred McGriff and Ryan Klesko, in the seventh inning on eight straight pitches. I know it really disappointed the team. The score was 1-1 at the time, and we ended up losing a tough game, 3-2, and I felt really bad.

"Between that game and the next one I pitched (Game 5), I kept my mouth shut and took the heat from the press and different people, then came back and beat Maddux on three days rest. It was the best I pitched since my career-threatening surgery, my shoulder reconstruction, so I was very proud of the way I responded there."

Chuck Hinton

(Outfielder/first baseman/third baseman/
second baseman, 1965-67, 69-71)

As a part-time infielder-outfielder for the Indians from 1965-67, Chuck Hinton often served as an "advisor" to teammate Leon "Daddy Wags" Wagner, which he did one day as the two players took batting practice before a Saturday afternoon game.

"I don't know what I'm doing wrong," lamented Wagner. "I keep popping up."

"Here's what you're doing wrong," said Hinton with a straight face. "You're hitting the bottom half of the ball. Try putting two extra pairs of inner soles in your shoes. That will raise you up so that you meet the ball square, instead of hitting under it."

"Hey, that sounds good. I'll try it," said Wagner.

Gomer Hodge

*(First baseman/third baseman/
second baseman, 1971)*

After he delivered four straight hits, three as a pinch hitter in his first four at-bats for the Indians in 1971, Gomer Hodge proudly announced to reporters interviewing him: "Gollee, fellas, I'm batting 4.000!"

Luis Isaac

(Coach, 1987-91, 1994-)

"The funniest man I ever knew was Looie (Luis) Tiant. One time when he was pitching somebody hit a long fly to center field. Looie started yelling, 'Go foul! Go foul!' even though the ball was hit dead away to center and went for a home run.

"Another time we were playing in Detroit and, in the ninth inning, Bill Freehan was hitting, and Looie got two strikes on him, then he hung a breaking ball. Freehan hit a high fly to left field, and by the time the ball landed over the fence to win the game for Detroit, Looie was in the dugout and yelling, 'OK guys, let's go, the bus is leaving in 45 minutes.'"

Brook Jacoby

(Third baseman, 1984-91, 92)

"When *Sports Illustrated* put us on the cover (March 1987) and said the Indians were the coming team in the American League, we all were kind of surprised—and at the end it was very embarrassing, because we finished in seventh (last) place. We had some very good young players, but we didn't have the pitching to go with our offense. Rick Sutcliffe and Bert Blyleven had been traded to get the nucleus of some young hitters, and when you look at what they (Sutcliffe and Blyleven) did after they left Cleveland . . . well, they had pretty good careers. So we had a good ball club, but we were young. We weren't quite ready.

"Most of the guys knew that if we put a winner on the field the fans would come out, which they did at times. One year (1986) we were only one game out, behind Boston in August, when we came home from a trip and the Stadium was packed that whole weekend. It was a lot of fun playing there then.

"I think Andy Thornton said it best, that (at that time, early 1980s) there was no solid ownership (of the Indians), and by doing what we did on the field helped keep the ball club in Cleveland. I like to think that what we did back then helped make it possible for what's happening in Cleveland now, because that was a pivotal time, whether there was going to continue to be a team playing in Cleveland or not."

Tommy John

(Pitcher, 1963-64)

A southpaw whose career began with the Indians, Tommy John was traded after winning just two games (and losing 11) in 1963 and 1964, though he became one of baseball's most consistent pitchers with the Chicago White Sox (1965-71) and Los Angeles Dodgers (1972-74) before suffering arm trouble.

He underwent ligament transplant surgery—which has subsequently been called a "Tommy John operation" and resumed his career with the Dodgers (1976-78), New York Yankees (1979-82), California Angels (1982-85), Oakland (1985), and the Yankees again (1986-89), retiring after the 1989 season.

"When they operated I told the doctor to put a Koufax fastball in my arm," said John. "They did—but it was a Mrs. Koufax fastball."

Maybe so. But in the 14 seasons after his surgery, John won 164 games, for a career total of 288 (with 231 losses).

Alex Johnson

(Outfielder, 1972)

During his one season with the Indians, outfielder Alex Johnson had few friends among the media. He seldom consented to be interviewed, usually greeting reporters with profane remarks. Most of the time, after games, he sat facing in toward his locker, reading the same softcover book that he tried to keep out of the sight of others.

However, a player whose locker was adjacent to Johnson's, was able to see the book and once revealed, "It was an electronics book and, funny thing, every time I looked, Alex was on the same page . . . I don't remember seeing him ever turn a page."

Mike Kekich

(Pitcher, 1973)

When he was signed by the Los Angeles Dodgers in 1964, Mike Kekich was called "another Sandy Koufax." Not only was he left-handed, Kekich launched baseballs with approximately the same velocity as did Koufax.

However, Kekich's resemblance to Koufax ended early, even before his career was devastated by the most unique trade in baseball history.

In 1973, after Kekich was dealt to the New York Yankees, he and fellow southpaw Fritz Peterson traded wives, children, and houses. It sounded like a soap opera, but this was real. Marilyn Peterson became Marilyn Kekich, and Susanne Kekich became Susanne Peterson. Shortly thereafter, on June 12, 1973, Kekich was traded to the Indians, though the deal obviously had no effect on his pitching career, and at the end of the season, with a 2-5 record, Kekich was released.

In an attempt to analyze what happened, Kekich said, "I was desperately depressed. The last good thing I could do in my life was throw a baseball, and it, too, was leaving me. I had lost everything; my friends, my Yankee team, my family, and then my physical talent.

"Just warming up for a game I literally forgot how to breathe. I was afraid I was going to choke to death. I knew I wasn't ready to pitch. How could I control the flight of a baseball when I couldn't control myself?"

Bob Kennedy

(Outfielder, 1948-54)

It was called "a helluva story" by Bob Kennedy, one that never came out at the time it happened, in 1948, after the Indians lost the final game of the season. The loss dropped them into a tie with Boston, forcing a one-game playoff for the pennant.

"We were on the train, going to Boston to play the Red Sox the next afternoon, and I got into my berth and tried to go to sleep. After awhile (second baseman) Joe Gordon came by and asked if I was asleep. I said, 'Well, yeah, I was until now.' He said, 'I thought you'd want to know . . . you're playing tomorrow.'

"I said, 'That's great. I'm glad to hear that.' He said, 'I'm gonna take a sleeping pill, you want one?' I said I'd never had one, but since I was awake, I thought it would help me get back to sleep, so I told him to give me one.

"Next thing I know it's morning and it's quiet, real quiet. I pulled the curtain back and leaned out of my berth, but didn't see anybody. I looked down the aisle and there was Gordon, and a little farther down I saw (Bob) Feller.

But nobody else. I looked at my watch and it was eleven o'clock. Eleven o'clock in the morning, and the game was at one o'clock! The train was parked in the yard and everybody was gone. Everybody but Gordon, Feller, and me.

"So, Judas Priest, we got dressed, ran like a son of a gun and caught a cab to Fenway Park. On the way, Joe told the cabbie to stop at one of those little lunch stands.

He ran in, got three milkshakes with a couple of eggs in each of them, and jumped back in the cab. When we got to the park and walked in the clubhouse (Manager Lou) Boudreau looked at us and started to say something, but Joe put his hand over (Boudreau's) mouth and said to Lou, 'Not now . . . later.'

"Can you believe I almost missed the greatest game . . . the most important game of my career? Gordon and Feller, too."

Talking about Satchel Paige, Kennedy said, "Don't let anybody tell you that Satch was a clown, or that he wasn't a good pitcher, because he was. A very good pitcher. Most of the time he'd come to the ball park in a big limousine accompanied by a lady, and when we asked who she was, he'd say, 'That's my wife.'

"Well, I'll tell you, there sure were a lot of Mrs. Paiges in the American League that year."

Kennedy played for the Chicago White Sox before he was traded to the Indians in 1948, and later for Baltimore, the White Sox again, Detroit, and Brooklyn, but said his seven seasons with Cleveland were the best of his 16-year major league career.

"My wife used to say that, when we were in Cleveland, it was like being in Camelot. She was right. Especially in 1948."

Ralph Kiner

(Outfielder, 1955)

In 1955, upon joining the Indians after hitting .285 with 22 homers for the Chicago Cubs the preceding season, Ralph Kiner insisted that his salary be cut 40 percent, instead of 25 percent, the maximum allowed by major league rule. "Maybe I should go to a psychiatrist (but) this is not a grandstand play. I simply want my performance with the Indians to determine my future salary," he said.

Duane Kuiper

(Second baseman, 1974-81)

"Mark Fidrych (of the Detroit Tigers) didn't last long, only a few years (actually six), but I swear he was one of the goofiest guys I ever saw. But, goofy or not, he could really pitch, especially his first season (1976) for the Tigers.

"He used to talk to the ball . . . hold it up in front of him, look at it and talk to it, before he pitched it. This one night, during a game at the old Stadium, a couple of our

Duane Kuiper

guys got one of the balls between innings, and wrote on it, something like, 'You're a jerk,' and some profanity, stuff like that, hoping he would see it. We were just trying to get into his head, you know, hoping it would rile him up. But it didn't. He held the ball up in front of him, like he always did, looked at it, and then pitched it. It didn't have any effect on him, not that we could tell. And the pitch he made, as I recall, the batter didn't swing at it, and then the umpire threw the ball out. That's all there was to it. Fidrych didn't care."

"Most people don't remember the game in 1977 that I hit my home run—my only home run (in 3,378 at-bats)—and that Al Michaels was doing it on national television. Michaels, you know, was famous for what he said during the 1980 Olympics. When the U.S. hockey game team beat Russia, Michaels said, "Do you believe in miracles?'

"Well, he used that same line—'Do you believe in miracles?'—when I hit my home run, and that was three years before he said it in the Olympics.

"When I hit it, I probably was even more surprised than Michaels. It was in the first inning. Paul Dade had just struck out and I was the second batter. I got ahead, 1-and-0 on the count and, in all honesty, I almost didn't swing at the next pitch, the one I hit out. It was either a high fastball or a hanging slider, and I was more of a low ball hitter in those days. So, when I swung—and you've got to remember, before that I never experienced watching a right fielder turn around and go back—and when I saw the number on the back of the right fielder's shirt, I thought to myself, 'Wow! This might have a chance to go off the wall,' but it did better than that. It sailed out of the ball park.

"Buddy Bell was waiting for me at the plate and half the guys came out of the dugout to greet me. Then, when I got up to hit for the second time, Bill Melton was standing nearby in the on-deck circle and said, 'You're not going to use that bat again, are you?' I said, 'Yeah, why not.' And he said, 'You better put it away, save it, because you might never hit another one' which I didn't.

"Somebody retrieved the (home run) ball, and they threw it in for me to keep. I have it somewhere in my attic, though I don't exactly know where."

Frank LaBono

(Visiting team batboy, 1938-41)

"I got my job as the batboy for visiting teams at League Park and the old Stadium when I was 13 years old, and it's an experience I'll never forget as long as I live.

"It was during that season (on October 2) that Bob Feller struck out 18 batters against Detroit (setting a then-major league record). He got Chet Laabs five times, and when Laabs came back to the dugout after the fifth strikeout, he broke every one of his bats—five or six of them, even a couple of other guys' bats—he was so mad. Finally Hank Greenberg and a couple other guys grabbed him before he could do any more damage, although he'd already done plenty."

"A lot of players played cards in the clubhouse before and after games, but Luke Sewell, who managed the (St.

Louis) Browns and Bucky Harris (Washington Senators) wouldn't allow it. I think that was pretty wise, because I'd see guys get mad at each other during a card game.

"Connie Mack was a real gentleman. Everyone called him 'Mr. Mack.' During double headers he would not allow anybody to eat anything except ice cream. That's all he allowed. Just ice cream. And no food could be brought in, even after the game. Mr. Mack was a very nice man and always wore a high collar and a tie. I remember one day it was so hot my shirt was soaked with sweat in the first inning, but Mr. Mack still had that high collar, shirt and tie with a straw hat. I went to him and asked, 'Mr. Mack, aren't you hot?' and he laughed and said, 'No, young man, I'm always cool.'"

"My favorite player was Mickey Vernon, who played for Washington (1939-48) and then the Indians (1949, 50). He was such a gentleman, probably the most gentlemanly visiting player I knew. We still write to each other, and I see him if he comes into town. Of all the players my mother had me invite for dinner, Vernon was the only one who ever brought her a gift, a box of chocolates once. She liked him, too.

"I also liked Joe DiMaggio, maybe because we're both Italian. I know there's a book that came out recently that made him look pretty bad, but to me he was a good guy.

"In those days the players didn't tip a lot, because they didn't make a lot of money. Not like today. But some of them were very generous to me. Back then, brown and white, and black and white dress shoes—saddle shoes, I guess they call them—were very popular. Guys used to ask me to clean them up before they left the clubhouse, and when I did, they'd give me a couple of bucks."

"I was there in 1940 when somebody dropped a basket of rotten fruit and vegetables on Birdie Tebbetts' head. Birdie went into the stands after the guy and gave him a helluva going over. Old Birdie (who became the Indians manager in 1963) was as tough as they make them, until he got old.

"The Tigers went crazy the day (September 27) they beat Bob Feller and the Indians (2-0) to win the pennant in 1940. After the game I went into the clubhouse and they gave me three brand-new balls. My pay in those days usually was two brand-new balls and a couple of dollars each game. But that day they gave me three. I couldn't wait until I got back to the clubhouse and got everybody's name on them, and then I went out and sold the balls for 25 bucks apiece. Twenty-five bucks in those days was real big money. Don't forget, that was 1940. You wouldn't get 25 bucks in a week if you worked a regular job.

"It was the following year (1941) that DiMaggio's (consecutive game hitting) streak was stopped (at 56 on July 17) at the old Stadium. When DiMaggio came back to the dugout after he grounded out (to shortstop Lou Boudreau) in the eighth inning to go 0-for-4, he said he hoped the Indians would tie the game so he'd get another chance. They didn't, although they did score twice in the bottom of the ninth and cut the Yankees' lead to 4-3. That's the way it ended.

"Nobody, including Joe, said much afterward. Everybody just left him alone, stayed away from him, not because he was mad or anything, but just to give him a little privacy, respect. Even when he went into the shower, nobody showered with him. Finally, when he came out and was getting dressed, I heard him tell Lefty Gomez that he was glad it was over. I guess because of all the pressure that had been on him."

"It was in 1938, when I was 14 years old, that I played catch with Lou Gehrig at League Park. Here's how it happened: many of the New York players were arguing about something, and doing a lot of swearing in the dugout before a game one day. Lou didn't like to hear it, and he didn't want me to hear, so he said to me, 'C'mon, Frankie, get a glove and play some catch with me . . . let's get out of here. You shouldn't hear that kind of talk.' I said to him, 'OK, Mr. Gehrig,' and he said, 'I'm Lou to you, Frankie. Not Mr. Gehrig.' Imagine that! Me, Frank LaBono, playing catch with the great Lou Gehrig."

"When World War II started, I went into the Navy and served aboard the USS Lexington, an aircraft carrier, until we got torpedoed on May 6, 1942, in the battle of the Coral Sea and the ship went down. I swam away from it as far as I could and saw a rubber raft with 13 other men on it, and was able to get on it. We were on that raft five days and four nights before a submarine came and picked us up.

"I was in the Navy a total of 39 months, and was discharged in May 1946, but I didn't go back to work at the ball park. By then I guess I was too old to be a batboy."

Napoleon Lajoie

(Second baseman, 1902-14; Manager, 1905-09)

It was during spring training in 1908 that Napoleon Lajoie, then the player-manager of the Indians, was hit in the head during batting practice by a pitch thrown by an erratic rookie southpaw named Jack Graney.

That night Lajoie summoned Graney to his hotel room and told the pitcher, "They tell me that the place for wild men is out west. So, you're going west, kid, so far that, if you go any farther your hat would float. Here's your railroad ticket (to the Indians farm team in Portland, Oregon)."

Graney switched to the outfield that season and two years later made it back to the Indians as their regular left fielder until his retirement at the end of the 1922 season. Nine years later, in 1931, Graney became the radio voice of the Indians, a job he held for the next 22 years.

Frank Lane

(General Manager, 1958-61)

They called him "Trader Lane" and "Frantic Frank" because of the 49 deals involving 108 players he made while serving as general manager of the Indians for three-plus seasons. Lane's justification for his incessant wheeling and dealing, and scorn for holding special promotions to attract larger crowds: "If the team doesn't do well, the fans won't give a damn about Bugs Bunny. The only promotion I care about is getting one more run than the other team."

Neither would he admit to regretting any of his transactions. "The only deals that irked me are the ones I didn't make," he said.

Longtime Indians pitcher Mel Harder, who was the team's pitching coach from 1948-63, during Lane's tenure, said of the former general manager: "Lane was a wild man. He couldn't go to sleep at night without dreaming up a trade. He was always up to something, and we never knew what it was until after he did it. I can't say what kind of an effect Lane had on the team, except that I know the players didn't like him."

Hal Lebovitz

(Cleveland Plain Dealer sportswriter)

"I liked Dale Mitchell a lot, though I didn't especially like the way he played ball. He was a slap hitter and didn't have a very good throwing arm, although he always hit for a high average. One day he put it all together—all the negative things. He didn't pull the ball when he should have and made a couple of weak throws from left field, so I ripped him—well, criticized him—in the paper.

"Several players told me the next day that I shouldn't go near Mitchell, because he was angry at me. But I felt it was important that I give him a shot at me, as I always did after I criticized a player. So I went up to him in the clubhouse and he seemed to be as nice as could be.

"He asked me, 'How are you, Hal?' I told him I was fine. Then he asked, 'Do you have a brother?' I was pleased that he wasn't mad anymore, and said, 'Thanks for asking, and, yes, I do have a brother.' Then he said, 'Well, he can go to hell, too.' "

Bob Lemon

(Pitcher, 1941-42, 46-58)

A Hall of Fame pitcher whose 15-year major league won-lost record for the Indians was 207-128, Bob Lemon managed the Kansas City Royals from 1970-72, Chicago White Sox in 1977 and 1978, and the New York Yankees in 1978 and 1979, and again in 1981 and 1982.

"I liked managing when I was doing it, when everybody got along all right," he said. "But everything changed. The animals began to run the zoo. It's not the same. Now a manager is expected to motivate his players, and that, to me, is ridiculous. Why should somebody need to be motivated to make a million dollars? Isn't a million dollars enough motivation?"

Originally a third baseman-outfielder who became a pitcher in 1946, Lemon said, "What would I have done if I had not switched to pitching? I don't know . . . but I probably wouldn't have lasted long in baseball. If I had learned to hit the change up, it might have been different. Hell, I'd run halfway to the mound trying to hit one, that's how bad it was for me.

"I could hit anything else they threw at me, but not the change up, and the word got around pretty quick. Pretty soon that's all I saw. Fastball out of the strike zone. Curve ball out of the strike zone. Then the damned change up."

Of his pitching career, during which he was a 20-game winner seven times: "The two most important things in life are good friends—and a strong bullpen." And, "I had my bad days on the field, but I didn't take them home with me. I left them in a bar along the way."

A key player in helping the Indians win the American League pennant and World Series in 1948, Lemon said of his teammates, "We were uninspirable . . . we already had all the inspiration we needed. That's what kept us so loose, all of us, all season. When we went out on the field we felt we were going to win all the time."

And how he would like to be remembered as a pitcher? "That I was awful brave to go out there with the stuff I had . . . and lucky."

Eddie Leon

(Shortstop/second baseman, 1968-72)

"It was either 1969 or 1970 when one day Sam McDowell came into the locker room and everybody knew he'd had a problem—a typical Sam McDowell problem— the night before. He had a little chunk of hair missing in the back of his head . . . there might even have been stitches, though I'm not sure.

"Anyway, Sam walked past Larry Brown, who could be very sarcastic in a kidding way, and Brownie said, 'Sam, would you please replace your divots?'"

"It's great to see the Indians doing so well now. What a difference—in both the team and the ball park—from when I played. Like I told Looie Tiant, 'I'm embarrassed when people talk about how bad we were in 1969.' He said, 'Yeah, but you can't blame it all on me,' and I said, 'I was only there for half of the season, so nobody can blame it all on me either."

Johnny Lipon

(Coach, 1968-71; Interim manager, 1971)

In 1969, when Johnny Lipon was a coach for the Indians, a Japanese team, the Hiroshima Carp, shared the Tribe's spring training facilities in Tucson, Arizona.

Early one morning that spring Lipon went to the clubhouse at Hi Corbett Field before the players were scheduled to report and was shocked at what he saw going on in the trainer's room.

There, with five or six members of the Japanese team surrounding him on the treatment table was Sam McDowell with several needles sticking out of his back and shoulder. Lipon screamed, "What the hell is going on in there! Leave that guy alone and get the hell out of here!"

The Japanese were administering an acupuncture treatment for McDowell, who had complained of a sore shoulder—but Lipon said later he thought the pitcher was being harmed, maybe even tortured.

Joe Lis

(Outfielder, 1974-76)

It was mid-April, 1974, and the Indians were playing in Milwaukee when rain halted the game in the fourth inning, delaying it for nearly an hour. Rusty Torres, an Indians outfielder, was in the bullpen beyond the right-field fence when the storm hit, and remained there for about a half an hour waiting for the weather to clear.

Also waiting for the rain to stop was Joe Lis in the dugout with several teammates and members of the Brewers grounds crew, when a fan, who'd had too much to drink, jumped out of the field boxes and ran onto the tarpaulin covering the infield. The grounds crew raced out of the dugout like a pack of police dogs to apprehend the interloper, which motivated several other fans to do the same—and for the grounds crew again to react accordingly.

Finally, when order was restored and, as the rain continued to fall, Torres decided to leave the bullpen and join his teammates. He climbed over the outfield fence and, carrying a bat, trotted across the field toward the dugout.

Lis, seeing Torres running in, prodded the grounds crew to "go after him like you did those fans" who'd invaded the field.

"Oh, no . . . he's got a bat in his hands, and he might swing it at us," the grounds crew chief said.

Lis told him, "Well, go after him like a curveball and he'll miss you."

Al Lopez

(Catcher, 1947; Manager, 1951-56)

"One time during the early 1950s—I don't recall exactly what year it was—we were playing in New York, and I got a call from (general manager) Hank Greenberg. He told me, 'A couple of your guys were out until 3 in the morning.'

"I asked him, 'Who were they and how do you know?'

Greenberg said, 'I can't tell you that. It's confidential. But you'd better find out and crack down.'

"I figured out right away who it probably was—Mike Garcia, who'd shut out the Yankees that night and probably was out celebrating his victory. I called him in and he admitted he was at a popular restaurant with teammate Johnny Berardino having a leisurely dinner. I told Mike, 'I would have given you permission. Just ask me next time.'

"He told me, 'Skip, we weren't doing anything wrong. In fact so-and-so was there. You can ask him. He was there with some blond.' (Lopez declined to identify the 'so-and-so,' but he indicated it was one of the team's high-moraled executives.)

"I later told Greenberg that I knew how he found out, and he never mentioned it again."

"One of the funniest things that happened when I managed the Indians—though I'm not sure you should write about it—involved a back-up catcher, Earl Averill Jr., whose father was the Hall of Fame outfielder for Cleveland.

"(Earl Jr.) was one of those mischievous guys who was always playing tricks on somebody, doing stuff like that for

Al Lopez

fun. So, this one game (in 1958) we were getting beat and Averill was in the bullpen warming up pitchers. I needed a pinch hitter, so I told (coach) Tony Cuccinello to get on the phone and bring Averill in, that he was going to bat the next inning. So, Averill came in and was sitting in the dugout, waiting to go up to hit. All of a sudden everybody in the dugout scrambled down to the other end, leaving Averill sitting there alone.

"What happened was that he'd let out the stinkingest fart you ever smelled. I looked around and asked what the hell was going on, and there was Averill looking at them and laughing. I finally realized what had happened, that he'd probably done it on purpose, and sent him back to the bullpen. About three days later we shipped him to San Diego (in the Pacific Coast League).

"Not too long ago, I saw Earl and kidded him that he farted himself out of the big leagues. He still insisted it wasn't him who did it—though I still think it was."

"If I had to pick one of all the guys I've had to pitch the seventh game of a World Series, I'd have to go with either Bob Lemon or Early Wynn. I think Wynn had better control than Lemon, but Lemon had better stuff. The problem with Lemon was his control. His fast ball was so alive, there were times he had trouble controlling it. But I would feel confident starting either one of those guys. Bob Feller, too, though his biggest years with the Indians were before I got to Cleveland.

"I know Feller wanted to start one of the games in the 1954 World Series (when the Indians were swept by the New York Giants), though we never really talked about it. It was just a decision I made (to come back with Lemon in the fourth game). If we had won the first or second game in New York, I was going to start Feller in Cleveland in the fourth game. But when we didn't (win either game in New York), why in hell was I going to pitch Feller? He was the fifth starter on the club at that time, and wasn't the Feller he'd been (earlier in his career).

"I had great respect for Feller. I idolized him. He was a great pitcher. One of the best in baseball for a long time. But by then (1954), Feller was going down hill."

John Lowenstein

(Outfielder/infielder, 1970-77)

Early in John Lowenstein's career with the Indians, he was asked if he'd like to see a banner in his honor hung at the old Stadium. Lowenstein reacted as if he'd been shot. "Basically, I'm against all banners. If somebody puts up a sign about me, I'd immediately disqualify myself from the game. Signs have no ethereal value."

And when it was suggested that a fans club be formed in his honor, Lowenstein instead created what he called an "apathy club" about which, he said, "Nobody knows how many members it has, because nobody is interested enough to show up for meetings."

John Lowenstein

Dino Lucarelli

*(Indians publicity/
public relations director, 1967-75)*

"John Lowenstein was one of my favorite players, even though he wasn't always the easiest guy to work with. Every year we'd send out questionnaires, and every year his would come back different. One year he said he was born in Great Falls, Montana, the next year he was born in Las Vegas, and so on. Every year it was something else.

"So was his nationality. One year he was Jewish, another year he was German-American. We never did know exactly what it was, though I never bothered to pressure him, because I probably wouldn't have gotten a straight answer anyway.

"Then, too, one year he would tell us his name should be pronounced Lowensteen, and the next it was Lowenstine. He drove the field announcers crazy, because he'd go up to one of them during a game and say, 'You're pronouncing my name wrong. It's not Lowensteen, it's Lowenstine. So the guy would change, and the next time we'd come to town he'd go to the field announcer and say, you are mispronouncing my name, and say just the opposite from what he had previously.

"And this one, which was a classic. One year (general manager) Phil Seghi set it up for Lowenstein to go to Venezuela to play winter ball. But we hadn't heard from him, and the general manager in Venezuela told Seghi that John never reported. We tried to reach him by phone and telegraph, but never could. Finally, I got a postcard from him. It said, 'Dear Dino. Here I am trying to hit the old apple in

Venezuela. The Chinese people here are great, but the Chinese food isn't so hot. John.'

"That was it. I took it in to Seghi . . . which is how we found out that he finally reported."

Another Lowenstein story: "One night we were on the road, and Lowenstein had a single room next to Buddy Bell and Jack Brohamer, who shared a room. Buddy and Brohamer were watching a movie on TV, and when there was a commercial break they went down the hall to the pop machine, leaving the door to their room open. While they were gone, Lowenstein sneaked into their room and hid in the closet. He stood there like a zombie and closed the door. When Bell and Brohamer come back, they sat down to watch the rest of the movie, and then went to bed. Bell opened the closet door, and there was Lowenstein standing there, his eyes closed and arms folded across his chest. Buddy screamed . . . he was scared to death. Lowenstein laughed and laughed."

Another character—and because he was, he also was a favorite of Lucarelli—was Joe Lis, who also was a favorite of then-manager Ken Aspromonte, even though Lis was only a substitute. "One time we were getting beat, like, 7-0, in the seventh inning," recalled Lucarelli, "and Aspromonte, who especially appreciated Lis for his rah-rah spirit in the locker room, hollered down the bench to Lis, 'Joe, do something. Get these guys worked up when they come off the field.' So, as the players came in, Lis knelt down on the top step of the dugout, took off his hat and started making the sign of the cross."

"Here's how bad things were back then. One night we were getting beat bad, something like 11-0 going into the bottom of the seventh inning. Johnny Singer, who was the leader of the band that played between innings, got on the microphone and said to the fans, 'C'mon, everybody, let's sing 'Take Me Out To the Ball Game'. But instead of singing, the crowd, which was unusually large for those days, started booing.

"Another time we were playing Baltimore and, when Ken Singleton struck out, the organist played, 'Bye, Bye, Blackbird.' Gabe Paul went crazy. He called down and had the organist fired, then and there, right on the spot."

"One year Gabe had a new Cadillac and, when he got to 1,000 miles, he told (handyman) Joe Botta to take the car back to the dealer for a checkup. So Joe did. But while he was driving to the dealer, he lit a cigar, wasn't paying attention and went through a caution light. He got broadsided, and Gabe's new Cadillac was demolished. Totaled. It was a miracle that Joe wasn't killed, though Gabe probably wished he had been.

"At the time it happened, Gabe was holding court in the Wigwam (media dining room) after lunch, with five or six reporters, when Joe called him on the phone to tell him the car was demolished. Gabe sat there in front of all of us and, as nice as he could be—which was very nice when the media was watching—was saying into the phone, 'Uh, huh . . . yes . . . OK,' and then, still sweetly, 'Thank you, and good bye.'

"He hung up the phone and, totally unruffled, continued to tell his favorite stories, reminiscing about all the guys he knew in the old days. Finally, one by one, all the reporters left and, as they were leaving, Gabe gave me one of his looks that meant I was supposed to stay put. Then, as soon as the last guy left and he heard the elevator door close, he looked around the corner to make sure nobody was there, and started pounding his fist on the table and yelling, 'That no good son of a bitch . . . ,' and more, for five minutes, before I knew what was wrong.

"Finally he said what happened, and I had to be careful not to laugh. But it was funny as hell."

"Then there was the famous Jimmy Dudley-Bob Neal story. They were broadcast partners on the air, but hated each other and didn't speak to each other off the air. When Dudley suffered a heart attack in the mid-1960s, Neal was asked if he went to visit his partner in the hospital. Neal reportedly said, 'I tried to get in his room to pull the plug on him, but they wouldn't let me in.'"

Candy Maldonado

(Outfielder, 1990, 93-94)

"People started calling me 'Candy' in 1978 when I was playing rookie ball in Leftwich, Alberta, Canada, for the Dodgers. Everybody was having a rough time pronouncing my first name—which is Candido—so I just cut it in half and let them call me Candy. That's how I got the name. But then, later, I told people it was because my mother thought I was so sweet."

"When I played for John McNamara in Cleveland (in 1990)—I guess because I was a veteran—he allowed me to, sort of, initiate the rookies . . . make them dress up in weird clothes on road trips.

"So, one time when we were in Baltimore, I went to the Salvation Army and bought a bunch of old clothes for the rookies to wear. The funniest of them all was Alex Cole. We made him go through the airport terminal dressed in women's clothes—high heels with pink pants and a yellow suit coat, and a sanitary sock tied around his waist as a belt.

"The best part of it—for us but not for Alex—was that there were about a hundred people, family and fans of his from his home in West Virginia, and he had to walk out the front of Memorial Stadium in Baltimore to our bus in front of all those people. If he didn't, it would have cost him a $500 fine—and he also would have had to go to the bus in his underwear because we had taken all of his regular clothes."

Rick Manning

(Outfielder, 1975-83)

"I'll never forget Lenny Barker's perfect game against Toronto (May 15, 1981). As a no-hitter goes on, the anticipation doesn't really start building until the fifth or sixth inning. But in this case Lenny was getting better the longer he went. He didn't have a strikeout the first three innings, but wound up with 11, all of them from the fourth inning on. The slider he was throwing was vicious. Standing behind him in center field, as I was, I could see how it was breaking, and by the sixth inning I sensed the real possibility that he would throw a no-hitter.

"The funny thing is, in the dugout, when a guy is pitching a no-hitter, nobody wants to talk to him, and definitely not say anything about a no-no. But not with Lenny. I remember (third baseman) Toby Harrah and I were telling him along about the eighth inning, 'C'mon, you can do this.' We came right out and said it. He was very laid back about it and just kept going. Everybody could sense something was going to happen.

"I think he made only one mistake pitch the whole game, to Lloyd Moseby, in the middle innings. Moseby ended up hitting a rocket that went foul by about three feet, and then Barker got him.

"Normally there are some great plays made in a no-hitter, but not really in this one, which also proves how dominating Lenny was. Harrah went into the stands to catch a foul ball (in the fifth inning) and (second baseman Duane) Kuiper made a good back handed play in the sixth, but otherwise there was nothing close to a hit.

"By the time the Blue Jays sent Ernie Whitt up as a pinch hitter, with two out in the ninth—I don't remember how the first two batters were retired—I'm thinking, 'I want this baseball.' It could be in right field or left field; I was going to catch that ball no matter where it went.

"Lenny went to a 1-and-2 count on Whitt, and I'm saying to myself, 'C'mon, let's go, either strike him out or make him hit the ball to me.' Whitt swung and hit the ball in the air and I was calling for it before it even went out of the infield. It was a very easy catch.

"People have asked me, was I nervous? You don't have time to be nervous. I mean, your awareness is so much more heightened because it was a perfect game. Imagine that! A perfecto! Only the eleventh in the history of baseball (at that time)."

Charlie Manuel

(Coach, 1988-89, 94-99; Manager, 2000-)

"During the 2000 season, when we were having so many injury problems and had to use 32 pitchers (a major league record), I went out to the mound to make a change. I said to the pitcher, 'OK, Bill . . . ', and he looked at me real funny and said, 'My name isn't Bill, it's Mike, Mike Mohler.' I said, 'OK, Mike, I'm glad to meet you, but I'm still going to make a change.' "

"I was playing in Japan one year and hit a line drive that hit the pitcher and broke his shoulder. The next year that same pitcher hit me. I went out after him, and he ran into my dugout and hid behind the manager. I couldn't get at him, but I was yelling at him, and finally my interpreter came along and said, 'Charlie, let him go. You've already scared him enough.' So I did.

"In Japan, if the Japanese sportswriters saw a blond woman in the stands, they'd write that it was my girlfriend. I'd tell them, 'She's not my girlfriend, but I'd like to meet her. Why don't you guys introduce me to her?' "

Manuel was the Indians' batting instructor before becoming the team's 37th manager in 2000. He played in the major leagues for Minnesota and the Los Angeles Dodgers, from 1969-75, and in Japan from 1976-81, then managed in the minor leagues the next six seasons, before joining the Indians' coaching staff.

Charlie Manuel

"In his 38-year professional baseball career, Manuel played with and against many great hitters. One in particular stands out, as he said upon taking over as manager of the Indians: "The more I see of Manny Ramirez, the more I believe he is the best right-handed hitter I've ever seen.

"Ramirez is such a good hitter because he is tension free. A couple of years ago, when we were coming out of spring training, Manny lost his suitcase. He was real upset because he had his gold necklaces in the suitcase and asked (clubhouse manager) Ted Walsh if he knew where his bag was. Walsh tracked it down and it turned out that Manny had left three or four paychecks in there. We're talking about big money, too. But Manny didn't care about that. He was just glad he had his gold necklaces back. That's why he can hit .400. He's tension free."

These are some Manuel-isms, a la Yogi Berra.

"We'll tackle that bridge when we get to it."

"If I'm going to use Wil (Cordero), I've got to start using him."

"When Russell (Branyan) is striking out, he's missing the ball a lot."

"I'm just going to let the chips fall where they lay."

"Sometimes people don't see what they are looking at."

"C.C.'s (Sabathia) problem is that he always has to throw a strike."

"We're just getting beat too early. It's like getting beat late or getting beat in the middle of the game. There are a whole lot of different ways to lose a game."

"I have two children and they both have degrees in English. After hearing their old man speak, I guess they figured they better learn English the right way."

Tom McCraw

(First baseman, 1972, 74-75; Coach, 1975, 79-82)

"One of the amazing things that happened when I was a coach here—and I'm still amazed when I think about it—was that one night Frank Robinson was in a full-blown argument with one of the umpires. I mean, the veins were popping in his neck, and all the profanity was coming out. Then the darnedest thing happened.

"While all this profanity and arguing is coming out of Frank's mouth, at the same time he is giving signs to his third base coach Dave Garcia, as to what he wanted the hitter to do.

"It also was almost as amazing to me that Garcia picked up the signs from Robinson as Frank was arguing with the umpire.

"When Frank finished arguing, I asked myself, 'What the heck did I just see?' I could hardly believe it, though I know it was true, because Garcia told me that what I saw was what was happening.

"I never saw anything like that in baseball before or since."

"Speaking of Robinson, he was very mentally tough and fought for what he wanted, what he thought was right. Now, when I see him in his job as vice president of on-field operations for the commissioner and dishing out all those fines, I call him the 'Hanging Judge,' because he's fining and suspending guys for doing the same things he always did as a player and manager.

"He was tough on umpires, but only if an umpire slacked off in his job. He expected everybody to do his job the way he tried to do his. And if you slacked off, whether you were an umpire or a coach or a player, he let you know about it."

Sam McDowell

(Pitcher, 1961-71)

"I think everybody in the ball park was shocked, including everybody on my team—though I wasn't—when Alvin Dark moved me from the mound to second base against the old Washington Senators (July 6, 1970, Cleveland Stadium). It didn't surprise me, because Alvin told me before the game that he might do it.

"We had a meeting and talked about what had happened in the previous game I pitched against the Senators. In that one, Frank Howard hit two home runs off me, and two other balls that should have been home runs, that almost killed our outfielders. I think Frank hit about .800 off me. I probably kept him in the big leagues for five or ten extra years.

"Alvin told me, 'Sam, I know you're a pretty good athlete, so this is what I'm going to do if you're pitching against Washington and the right situation presents itself. If Frank Howard comes up anytime after the seventh inning and we're either winning the game or one run behind, I'm going to take you out, bring somebody in to pitch to Howard, and then bring you back to close out the game.'

Sam McDowell

"I said, 'Fine, no problem.' But that's because I assumed he meant he'd put me in right field or first base, which I had played. If you recall, I was signed by the Indians as an outfielder and a pitcher.

"But this time, with Howard coming up with runners on second and third and two out, and we were ahead by two runs (4-2), Alvin came to the mound and said, 'Sam, you go to second base.' Then he switched (second baseman) Eddie Leon to third (replacing Graig Nettles), and brought Dean Chance in to pitch.

"Dark's plan was for Chance, a right-hander, to intentionally walk Howard, which would load the bases and bring another right-handed batter, Rick Reichardt, to the plate. That way, if the Senators substituted a left-handed pinch hitter for Reichardt, Dark could counter it by putting me back in to pitch.

"What happened was that Reichardt, with the bases loaded, batted against Chance and hit a sharp grounder to Leon, who—I guess, without thinking—scooped it up and fired it to second to me. His throw was a little low, and I dropped to my knees because I wasn't about to miss it, and it beat Howard as he came roaring into second for the third out.

"I went back to pitch the ninth inning and got them out (three strikeouts), and we won, 4-2 (giving him a 12-4 record).

"What's really interesting to me is that the rules state that a pitcher gets credit for a complete game if he's responsible for all 27 outs. Well, I made the out at second base, which means I was responsible for all 27, but I didn't get credit for a complete game, and I still want to know why not."

On September 18, 1966, McDowell was pitching what he later called "the game of my life" against the Tigers in Detroit. "I often wonder if I could have struck out 18 (and tied what was then the major league record) if I could have gone all the way . . . if I hadn't said anything to (interim manager) George Strickland . . . if he hadn't taken me out of the game.

"One thing I do know, I had everything that night. My fastball was as good as it ever was, and my control was nearly perfect. I got 14 strikeouts in only six innings. No matter what pitch I threw, I could put it anywhere I wanted. I was at my all-time best, and I don't think I was ever that good after that night.

"I went back to the dugout at the end of the sixth inning and told Strickland my arm was beginning to tighten. I only said it because I wanted him to have somebody ready, just in case. We were winning (5-1), and I didn't want to take any chances.

"I remember telling George, 'I'm OK, and I want to stay in there. But maybe you should keep somebody ready just in case.' Just like that, he took me out. I'd had some shoulder trouble early that season, and Strickland probably wanted to be sure I didn't hurt myself again.

"Nobody will ever know for sure what might have happened. But I only needed four more strikeouts to tie the record (then shared by Bob Feller and Sandy Koufax) and five to break it, and I had three innings to get them. That's why, of all the games I pitched, it's one I'll never forget."

By his own admission, McDowell was the biggest drunk in the major leagues during his too-brief pitching career with the Indians (1961-71), San Francisco (1972-73), New York Yankees (1973-74), and Pittsburgh (1975).

One night in Tucson, Arizona, in 1971, McDowell was arrested for drunk driving. The police offered to let McDowell out on bail in the wee hours of the morning to avoid media detection if Indians public relations director Ed Uhas would go to the jail and post bond.

When Uhas did, he was ushered into the cellblock where McDowell, still drunk, was clinging to the bars of his cell. Upon seeing Uhas, McDowell exclaimed, "Oh, no. Don't tell me they got you, too, Eddie."

Don McMahon

(Pitcher, 1964-66)

It was a very hot and humid afternoon in Cleveland during a game in July 1964, and Manager Birdie Tebbetts, angered by the players' complaints, threatened to impose a $50 fine against the next player who grumbled about the weather.

An inning later, as he came off the field, relief pitcher Don McMahon grabbed a towel to wipe the sweat off his face and said, "Jeez, it is so hot out there . . . ," and then, remembering Tebbetts' warning, quickly added, " . . . but I love it, Birdie, I love it. Honest, I do."

(He wasn't fined.)

Al Milnar

(Pitcher, 1936, 38-43)

"I don't remember too much about it anymore, it was so long ago, but I'm the guy who gave up the hits that extended DiMaggio's streak to 56 (on July 16, 1941). The game was played at League Park, and the Yankees beat us, 10-3, before we (the Indians) stopped him the next night at the Stadium.

"Giving up the hit—actually, two of them (to DiMaggio)—bothered me, but what the hell, he hit in 55 games before that. The thing that bothered me more was that we lost the game.

"I always threw DiMaggio a lot of sliders, so it probably was a slider that he hit each time. In those days the slider was kind of an unknown pitch. In fact, Phil Rizzuto once told me that I was the first guy who ever threw him a slider."

Orestes "Minnie" Minoso

(Outfielder, 1949, 51, 58-59)

"I liked Frank Lane. I liked him a lot. I used to call him 'Papa No. 2,' and he used to call me and say, 'I want to speak to my son, Minnie Minoso.' So somebody would come over to me and say, 'Some crazy guy on the phone wants to talk to you. He say to tell you that your daddy No. 2 wants to talk to you,' which is why I call him my Papa No. 2. He treated me good. Like a papa.

"One time he even introduced me to his daughter. He say to her, 'This is your brother, and I am his Papa No. 2.'

"Lane was a good man. I know a lot of people in Cleveland did not like him, but I loved him. People no like him because he tell the truth, and anything he thinks is good, he'd do it. Even trade Rocky (Colavito). He thought it was a good deal, so he did it."

Fernando Montes

(Strength coach, 1993-)

"On one of our flights I overheard Pat Borders (a Tribe catcher 1997-99) say that he'd never been embarrassed during his major league career. Several of the players also took note of it and decided they wanted to do something about it.

"A few days later when Pat was going to play in a Saturday afternoon game, I talked to the guys in the scoreboard room where they play introduction music for each player as he comes up to bat. I asked if they had anything from the old 'Hee-Haw' TV program, or some music like that, and they said they'd find something. I told them to play it when Borders stepped into the batter's box for his first at-bat.

"When he did, they played the theme song from 'Green Acres.' He looked into the dugout, and Kevin Seitzer and I are literally falling down laughing. And to make it even better—or worse for Pat—the catcher, Mike MacFarlane, turned to Pat and said, 'I hope that's your favorite song.'

"Pat struck out and came back to the dugout, threw his helmet down and told us, 'You tell the guys up there that if they play that music again I'm going to kill somebody.'"

Ray Murray

(Catcher, 1948, 50-51)

"I loved Bill Veeck, though I probably should have hated him. He had me up and down, between Cleveland and Oklahoma City like a damned yo-yo in 1948.

"When I was called back to the Indians in September, my wife Jackie and I got into town around three in the morning, went to bed, and about eight o'clock the phone rang, waking us up.

"It was Veeck. He said, 'I want you and the wife in my office in 30 minutes,' because there was something he wanted to talk to me about.

"We were staying at the Hotel Cleveland (now the Renaissance Hotel on Public Square) and I told him, 'Hell, Bill, we've been traveling and we're tired. I'll come down later.' He said, 'No, I want to see you right away. Take a cab. I'll pay for it.'

"Well, he was the boss and what could I do? I didn't want to hurt my chances, so Jackie and I got dressed and took a cab to the Stadium. I didn't expect to be there long, so I told the cabbie to wait.

"When we got to Veeck's office, he said, 'I appreciate the way you people have cooperated with me and I want to do something for you.'

"He held up a key and said, 'This is for a new Pontiac car. If you can find it, it's yours,' though he wouldn't tell me where to even look. He was laughing, but I knew he wasn't joking.

"Then I remembered, from when I was up with the club earlier in the season, that (Veeck) did business with a car dealer on the west side. I think it was called 'West Side Pontiac.' So Jackie and I jumped back in the cab and told him to take us there.

"We went in the showroom and there's a new Pontiac sitting over in the corner. I asked the salesman if I could try my key in the ignition, and when I did, VAROOM! The car started. How about that! We drove it out the door.

"It had to be worth about $4,800 at least. When the season ended, after the World Series, we drove that Pontiac home and kept it for a long time, all because I 'cooperated' with Bill, which means I didn't cuss and raise hell every time they sent me down.

"So, sure, I loved Bill Veeck. Why wouldn't I?"

Ray Narleski

(Pitcher, 1954-58)

It all began for Ray Narleski, one of baseball's first relief specialists in 1953 when he was pitching in the minor leagues for Indianapolis of the Class AAA American Association.

"It was strange the way it happened," he said. "I had lost a 12-inning game and was determined to find out what I'd done wrong. So I went out to pitch batting practice the next day, and a couple days later Birdie Tebbetts, who was the manager, said he wanted to talk to me. At first I thought he was calling me in for an attitude kind of thing, you know?

"But he said, 'Ray, I'm going to make you a reliever.' I said, 'The hell you are,' because, back then, relievers were old guys, guys who weren't good enough to be starters. Birdie said, 'No, this (becoming a reliever) can take you up to the big leagues.' He said he remembered seeing me throw the ball past Luke Easter and other good hitters in spring training, and said, 'You can throw it high and tight and low and away, and blow them away, which is a great thing.'

"It turned out he was right, and that it was good for me. No, make that very good."

"How hard did I throw? Well, I'll tell you. When I see these guys on TV and they say they are throwing 95 (mph), I know there were times when I could go into my full windup that I must have gone into the 100s. I know I did, compared to the 95s they say these guys are throwing. I could feel the ball explode right out of my hand. I really could. Boom! I could feel I had it. And I could go a long way, too. Not just one or two innings.

"I always wanted to be a starter, because starters get paid better than relievers. But looking back on it, I don't have any great regrets because I had a good career in Cleveland." (If saves were counted during Narleski's time as they are now, he would have had 13 in 1954 and 19 in 1955.)

Graig Nettles

(Third baseman, 1970-72)

When the Indians played in Cleveland's old Municipal Stadium with its 80,000-plus seating capacity, crowds were sparse in what was known as the "bad old days"—the 1960s through the 1980s. That included 1970-72, when Graig Nettles was one of the best third basemen in baseball.

Nettles also was known for his witty remarks, such as the time he was asked by a fan, "What time does tomorrow's game start?"

Nettles replied, "Well . . . what time can you make it?"

Satchel Paige

(Pitcher, 1948-49)

When Bill Veeck signed Satchel Paige to pitch for the Indians on July 7, 1948 the venerable J. G. Taylor Spink, publisher and editor of *The Sporting News*, ridiculed it as a cheap publicity stunt.

"To bring in a pitching 'rookie' of Paige's age (then thought to be 42) casts a reflection on the entire scheme of operations in the major leagues," Spink wrote in an editorial. He claimed it would "demean the standards of baseball in the big circuits," and that, "if Paige were white, he would not have drawn a second thought from Veeck."

Satchel Paige

Paige, who went 6-1 with a 2.48 earned run average to help the Indians win the pennant and World Series in 1948, tended—by his own statements—to agree with Spink.

"People don't come to see the ball game," he said early in his brief career with the Indians. "They come out to see me strike out everybody. Occasionally I didn't."

However, after Paige pitched a three-hitter to beat the Chicago White Sox, 1-0, on August 20, Veeck fired off a telegram to Spink—and made it public—that said: "Paige pitching. No runs, three hits. He definitely is in line for *Sporting News* rookie of the year award.

"Regards, Bill Veeck."

Legendary were Paige's stories of the old Negro leagues, in which he pitched for more than two decades before getting his chance with the Indians. Of his former teammate, "Cool Papa" Bell, Paige said, "One time he hit a line drive right past my ear. I turned around and saw the ball hit his behind, sliding into second, that's how fast he was."

When the subject of his advanced years was raised, Paige insisted, "Age is a question of mind over matter. If you don't mind, it doesn't matter."

Once, at the end of Paige's career and the beginning of Nolan Ryan's, the old-timer asked Ryan if he knew what the best pitch was. Ryan recounted their conversation. "I said, 'Fastball?' and Paige said, 'No, the bow tie.'

"'The bow tie? What's the bow tie?' I asked Paige," said Ryan. "Satch told me, 'Fastball, right here,' and drew his hand across his neck. In other words, high and tight. That was my lesson from Satchel Paige a long time ago."

And Paige's rules for staying young: "Avoid fried meats which angry up the blood; if your stomach disputes you, lie down and pacify it with cool thoughts; keep the juices flowing by jangling around gently as you move; go very light on the vices, such as carrying on in society (because) the social ramble ain't restful; avoid running at all times; and don't look back, something might be gaining on you."

Gabe Paul

(President/General Manager, 1963-72, 78-86)

After joining the Indians as part owner, president, and treasurer in 1963, Gabe Paul remained at the helm of the club in one capacity or another until 1972. He left to join George Steinbrenner as president of the New York Yankees, serving in that position for seven years.

When F.J. "Steve" O'Neill purchased controlling interest in the Indians in 1979, Paul returned to Cleveland as the chief executive officer of the team. He did so, Paul said, because, "Cleveland is a sleeping giant. Give the fans a winning team and they'll flock to the Stadium as they did in the past."

One of Paul's best deals was the acquisition of pitcher Gaylord Perry (along with shortstop Frank Duffy) in a November 29, 1971 deal with the San Francisco Giants for pitcher Sam McDowell. Of the criticism Perry regularly faced because of accusations that he threw a spitball (or 'grease ball'), Paul said, "Gaylord Perry is an honorable man. He only uses the spitter when he needs it."

Mike Paul

(Pitcher, 1968-71)

"It was 1970 or 1971, and we're playing Washington at the old Stadium, and Darold Knowles is pitching against us. He threw one at Graig Nettles' head that knocked him down and Graig was pissed. He swung at the next pitch, missed it, and threw his bat at the mound. Knowles had to jump to get out of the way of it. So all of us in the dugout started to charge out, thinking there's going to be a brawl. But Frank Howard, who was playing first base for the Senators, yelled out, 'Hold it! Stop right now.'

"Well, you know how big Frank Howard is (6-7, 260). They called him the 'Washington Monument,' and when he yelled, 'Hold it!' you never saw so many guys freeze on the top step of the dugout. Then he said, 'That's one for you and one for us. Now let's play ball.' Which we did."

"Another time, it was during the 'Year of the Tiger' (1968) and it was my first trip into Detroit. We were in the eighth or ninth inning of the game, and I'm in there in relief and here comes a tough right-handed hitter, though I can't remember who it was. Alvin Dark came out and said he wanted me to go play first base. I said, 'What!' And he said, 'Yeah, I want you to play first base for one hitter while I bring in Stan Williams. Then I'll bring you back in to face Jim Northrup, or one of their other left-handed batters.

"So, I'm standing over at first base, and Emmett Ashford, the umpire, said, 'Make sure you keep your foot on the base.' I told him, 'Emmett, I just hope they hit a fly ball. I don't want any part of this.' People were yelling at me —remember, I was a rookie—and I was flat-out scared I was going to screw up.

"The batter got a base hit or something, and that was it. I went back to the mound and, because Dark took out Tony Horton for me to play first base, we didn't have another first baseman. Lee Maye, an outfielder, had to go to first base—and you can imagine what happened next.

"Northrup hit my first pitch, a slider, on the ground to Maye, and he botched it. It's like they always say, when you're playing out of position, the ball will always find you.

"It didn't find me at first base that night, but it sure as hell found Maye, and we lost the game because it did. That was the only time I played first base, thank God. I don't know if Maye ever did again."

"The first two spring trainings I was with the Indians, 1968 and 1969, Alvin Dark just made sure that everybody got in shape gradually. He didn't want anybody pulling any muscles, or getting hurt from doing too much. So we'd run maybe 10 foul lines—foul pole to foul pole—at maybe three-quarter speed, no all-out effort. Alvin wanted everybody to get into shape gradually. So we did that.

"The next year, when some of us got in early for spring training, everybody was kind of doing the same lollygagging, foul pole to foul pole thing, just taking it real easy, the way we did the year before.

"But then Dark came in and said, 'OK boys, we're going to change things this year. I want everybody to run three miles under 21 minutes, and I want you to keep running it every day until you can do it in 21 minutes.' Everybody started complaining that we weren't ready for it because we weren't expecting it, but we still had to do it.

"So, this one day I was running with Sam McDowell. Everybody took off. One of the coaches clicked the stop watch and, boom! Sam started running like a bat out of hell. But once he got to the far side of the field where it was out of sight from Alvin and the coaches, he pulled a pack of cigarettes out of his back pocket, lit one and stood there smoking as everybody went running by. Next trip around, Sam, after flat-out skipping a lap, joined us and was laughing like hell. I'm sure Alvin found out, but he never did anything.

"Sam got away with it ... if you could pitch the way he could, you could get away with a lot of things."

Gaylord Perry

(Pitcher, 1972-75)

Opposing teams often charged that Gaylord Perry threw spitballs—or "grease balls"—and the complaints actually pleased the pitcher. Though he never completely denied the accusations, he teased his critics, saying, "I don't throw illegal pitches. I just leave a lot of evidence lying around."

Ken Aspromonte, Perry's manager, was not so subtle when he was asked the obvious question. "He'd throw it three, four times to each batter, especially with men on base," Aspromonte said. "He put this jelly on the ball that was a light film. It looked almost like sweat. He kept it hidden on his glove, chest, arm, neck and uniform. He had cartons of the stuff. It would make the ball either sink or take off."

Frank Duffy, the Indians shortstop then, was another who confirmed that Perry threw grease balls. Duffy said, "If you touched the spot where the grease was, you couldn't control the ball," and that he changed his normal throwing grip whenever Perry pitched.

On September 27, 1974, when the Indians acquired Frank Robinson—as a player, General Manager Phil Seghi emphasized—Perry was outspoken in his objection to the addition of the future Hall of Famer.

And Robinson was equally outspoken when he reported to the clubhouse for the game that night against the New York Yankees.

Earlier in the day Perry was quoted in the *Plain Dealer* that he wanted to be paid in 1975 "the same salary, plus a dollar more" than the $173,500 that Robinson was receiving as a part-time player.

Robinson wasted no time confronting Perry as the two men dressed for the game, and they had to be separated by Aspromonte. It launched a volatile relationship between the two men that was not rectified until June 13, 1975 when Robinson, then the manager of the Indians, and Seghi traded Perry to the Texas Rangers for pitchers Jim Bibby, Jackie Brown and Rick Waits, and a reported $100,000.

Jim Perry

(Pitcher, 1959-63, 74-75)

"One of the games I remember so well was in 1960, Ted Williams' last year. I was pitching against the Red Sox and had a 1-0 lead going into the ninth inning and, to win the game, 1-0, the three guys I had to get out were Jackie Jensen, Frank Malzone and Williams. I got the first two without any trouble, but Williams was a little different. I was still throwing pretty good, 94 (mph), but he kept pulling my pitches—even those on the outside—foul to right field.

"I finally got him on my fourth pitch, but it wasn't easy. He hit my fast ball to right field. I turned and saw Tito Francona take one step in, but suddenly realized he shouldn't have—and jumped up and caught the ball. We were lucky on that one, and we won."

"People always ask me what it was like to pitch against my brother Gaylord. The first time we did was in 1970, in the All-Star Game. I was with Minnesota then, and Gaylord was pitching for San Francisco. I pitched two innings, the seventh and eighth, and gave up one run, and Gaylord pitched the sixth and seventh and also gave up one run. They (the N.L.) got a run in the ninth off Catfish Hunter and won, 5-4.

"The same thing happened three years later (in 1973), the only time we started a championship game against each other, when I was pitching for Detroit and Gaylord for the Indians. I was ahead by two runs after six innings, but Cleveland tied it in the seventh and neither of us finished the game—and neither of us was the winner or loser.

"Something else people always ask was if there was a big rivalry between Gaylord and me. There really wasn't. We both went out there every day and did what we were supposed to do for our team, no matter who was pitching against us. That's the way we were. The way we were brought up by our father. I know I always tried to pitch competitively, the same way if I had a one-run lead or a ten-run lead.

"I got to the big leagues before Gaylord. My last season in the minors was in 1958 when I pitched for Reading (Pennsylvania of the Class A Eastern League). That was the year Gaylord signed with the Giants. He got a lot more money to sign than I did, but that was OK, because the money wasn't all that big when I started in pro ball (1956)."

"Gaylord used to drive the other teams—and the umpires—wild, the way he taunted them. Our clubhouse (at the old Stadium) and the umpires room were real close, separated only by a short stairway, and one of the things Gaylord did was sneak up to where they dressed and put white flour in the resin bag. Then, when he was on the mound and used the resin bag, he made sure a lot of the powder got all over his hand, and when he pitched the ball it would come flying out all over the place which, most of the time, surprised the batter.

"We used to call it Gaylord's 'puff ball.' "

Hank Peters

(Farm Director/General Manager/
President, 1966-71, 87-91)

"After the 1970 season, which had been another difficult year for us, I was farm director and (owner) Vernon Stouffer met with the directors. They called me in and said the budget had to be cut, and it was going to be a very big cut, including between a 35 and 40 percent cut in our player development. And to make it even worse, we hadn't been spending that much money to begin with. It meant some major amputations had to take place.

"The directors didn't tell me what I had to do, they just told me this is how much money you are going to have, and it wasn't much.

"Vernon asked, 'Is this going to hurt us very much?' I asked him, 'Well, before I answer, let me ask, are you going to keep this ball club?' He bristled a little bit, then said, 'Why do you ask that question?' I told him, 'The things you do and don't do today, in player development, are never reflected immediately. So, if you intend to sell the club in the next two or three years, you don't need to be concerned. On the other hand, if you intend to keep the ball club, well, then you are committing suicide by cutting our player development budget as drastically as you are planning to do.'

"Which is what happened. He sold the club two or three years later, and when I think back on it, it was a nightmare.

"Vernon wasn't very happy when I told him what I did. But I was at the point where I didn't give a damn. We cut two or three minor league teams, leaving us with the minimum number, four, that Major League Baseball said we had to have, we eliminated all but eight or nine scouts, from about 16 or 18, which we'd been building up gradually, trying to improve, and which had helped us make some improvements.

"At the time, before I was ordered to cut the budget, I felt we had finally begun to show some progress. But when the directors ordered the cut back, we ended up releasing 30 or 40 (minor league) players, several of whom caught on with other clubs and made it to the big leagues.

"And that, in my opinion, is what happened to the Indians, in what you guys in the media call the 'bad old days.' "

"Something else that contributed to the decline of the franchise in those days occurred in 1969, on July 4, to be exact. Stouffer put Alvin Dark in charge of all player personnel matters as both the general manager and manager, and took the GM duties away from Gabe Paul.

"At the time it happened, I was in the Carolinas, visiting one of our minor league teams, and I got a call from Stouffer. I told him I'd be returning to Cleveland in a few days, and he told me to meet him, that he had some thing he wanted to discuss with me.

"I did, and he dropped it on me. He said, 'I am making some changes. Gabe will continue as president, but won't have anything to do with the players. Alvin is going to run everything as general manager and field manager. He also told me that Dark didn't know a lot of things about being the general manager, and he wanted me to help him.

"As you can well imagine, I couldn't wait to get away from Stouffer to call Gabe. And when I did, Gabe, of course, was at wit's end. He called Alvin just about every name you could imagine, privately, of course. Publicly he kept telling you guys (in the media) that he was a 'happy warrior' for the next year or two, or however long the new arrangement lasted. To tell you the truth, I think I was the only one who kept Gabe sane during that time.

"As for me, I was between them all. I had Vernon Stouffer and his son Jim on one shoulder, Alvin on the other, and if I had three shoulders, Gabe would have been on that one. I often wondered, what did I do to deserve this? It was a comedy of errors, which was reason enough for me to get out."

(Peters left the Indians in 1972 and served as president of the minor leagues through 1975).

Jim Piersall

(Outfielder, 1959-61)

"They've taken all the color out of baseball. Guys like me and Billy Martin and Leo Durocher—colorful guys like that—could never play today. They wouldn't have us.

"When I played, we didn't need teachers. We learned things ourselves. Today, you have to teach. That's what it's all about. Kids don't play enough, and they don't have the equipment (talent) to be good outfielders. A lot of today's kids are also dreamers, not workers."

"I used to get really pumped up when we played in Yankee Stadium. One time Joe DiMaggio came up to me in a restaurant and said, 'Nobody gets them any better than you.' Willie Mays paid me the same kind of a compliment once. He said, 'Piersall is looney, but all he ever does is catch the ball.' "

Lou Piniella

(Outfielder, 1968)

The Indians re-acquired Lou Piniella from Baltimore in a minor league trade during the winter of 1965-66. They originally signed him out of high school in 1962, and in 1963 traded him to the old Washington Senators who, in turn, dealt him to the Orioles in 1964.

After the Indians obtained Piniella, Frank Lane, then general manager of the Orioles, predicted, "The fans in Cleveland will love Piniella, mark my words."

Why? "Because Piniella looks just like that dago fruit peddler, Rocky Colavito," whom Lane had traded to Detroit five years earlier, incurring the wrath of Tribe fans everywhere.

As it turned out, Piniella played three seasons (1966-68) in the Indians' farm system and made it to Cleveland for a brief trial in September 1968 when he appeared in six games without a hit in five at-bats. He was then claimed by Seattle in the 1968 expansion draft, but before playing a game for the Mariners, Piniella was traded to the Kansas City Royals and won the American League "Rookie of the Year" award in 1969.

Piniella recalled, "When I was playing for the Indians (Class AAA) farm club in Portland in 1967, I'd hit six or seven home runs early in the season, but I was batting only about .180. Johnny Lipon, our manager, called me into his office and asked if I wanted to stay in Portland or go down to Double-A ball. I told him I wanted to stay (in Portland), of course.

"The next day Lipon handed me a thick-handled, Nellie Fox model bat, and worked with me with that bat every day for the next several months. Until then I'd been strictly a pull hitter, but Lipon had me hitting only to right field or center the rest of the season.

"I ended up hitting .289, and because of Lipon's help I got to the big leagues in a couple of years. When I did, I told Lipon that he was the guy who helped me more than anybody.

"The ironic thing is that, Gabe Paul was the general manager in Cleveland when I was let go in the expansion draft, and knew how badly I wanted to make it to the big leagues with the Indians. And then, in 1974, when Gabe was president of the Yankees, he traded for me—so he must have remembered me."

Eric Raich

(Pitcher, 1975-76)

Upon being promoted by the Indians from their Class AAA Oklahoma City farm club in 1975, pitcher Eric Raich was asked to pose for a picture with Manager Frank Robinson and pitcher Blue Moon Odom.

"I feel like an Oreo cookie," said Raich, as he stood between Robinson and Odom.

Pedro Ramos

(Pitcher, 1962-64)

"If it happened today, I wouldn't be player of the week, I'd be the player of the month," said Pedro Ramos. He was talking about the Indians game on July 31, 1963, when he struck out 15 batters and hit two homers in a 9-5 victory over California. His second homer also was the second of four that were hit consecutively off Angels right hander Paul Foytack in the sixth inning. Woodie Held started the on-slaught, and Ramos's homer was followed by shots off the bats of Tito Francona and Larry Brown.

Rudy Regalado

(Third baseman, 1954-56)

"In the middle of the 1954 season, when we were fight-ing to win the pennant, we were scheduled—for some rea-son, I don't know why—to play an exhibition game in Jer-sey City against the Dodgers. It was a real hot and muggy day, and Al Rosen, our captain, complained especially loud about the weather, that it was so bad. There must have been a million mosquitoes buzzing around us that night, and our minds were on playing the Orioles in Baltimore the next night, not on a meaningless exhibition game in Jersey City.

"He suggested that we just go to the plate and hit the first pitch and get out of there as early as we could, which we did, and the game was played in only one hour and 35 minutes. We lost the game, 1-0, and I remember I went 0-for-4—hit the ball four times with four swings of the bat—but nobody cared."

"I guess I owe a lot to Bobby Avila for me being able to make the team in 1954. Avila was the Indians' second baseman then, and a good one, but was a holdout in spring training, though everybody said he had a visa problem getting out of Vera Cruz, Mexico. People nowadays just walk over the border, but then, well, I guess Bobby just wanted a big raise. At any rate, he was late getting to spring training.

"I was on the roster of one of the Indians' farm clubs and was planning to drive from my home in San Diego to Daytona Beach, where the minor league teams held spring training. I asked Hank Greenberg if it would be OK if I left home early and stopped off in Tucson en route to Florida so that I could get a couple of weeks of help from the Indians coaches (Red Kress and Tony Cuccinello). Hank approved and when I arrived in Tucson I suited up and worked out with the big team. I didn't have a position, but I took batting practice every day and hit the ball pretty good.

"Avila still wasn't in camp when the exhibition games began and Owen Friend, another infielder who was on the roster, had a bad leg, and Cuccinello asked me if I'd ever played second base. I said no, that I'd played third base, shortstop and the outfield, but never second base, though I'd sure be willing to do it if they needed someone. Tony worked with me for about an hour before the game—how to make the pivot on double plays and how to avoid the spikes of a runner sliding into second, that kind of thing—and I went out and played OK, even got two hits.

"The same thing the next day, and that was the start of a real hot streak for me. I hit 11 home runs and drove in 22 runs, and wound up with a .447 average that spring.

"Avila finally showed up, maybe because people began to say that he was losing his job to that Regalado kid, even though I was a third baseman, not a second baseman. After Bobby arrived in camp, the Indians found a place for me on the roster, and I never did go to Daytona Beach. Eventually Al Lopez put Rosen on first base, and I started the season at third.

"I don't know what happened that caused me to hit so well. If I knew, I would've stayed hot. I was just in a groove, like Tiger Woods gets in a groove and everything goes right. I stayed hot until about the middle of June and then they started throwing me that pitch . . . what do they call it? Oh, yeah. A curveball . . . and I cooled off in a hurry."

Kevin Rhomberg

(Outfielder, 1982-84)

"I don't know when or how it all began, but I was always a very superstitious guy, especially when I played ball.

"For some reason I felt it would be bad luck if somebody touched me, and I didn't touch him back. Don't ask my why, I just had to. It was really a superstition, though I've been called neurotic. Bert Blyleven thought I was crazy. Something else that was really important to me was that, wherever I went I'd never turn right, I'd always turn left. Even if I had to make three left turns to go right. Why'd I do it? Well, think about it. There are no right turns in baseball, are there?

"A sportswriter in Texas once asked Rod Carew—who also was very superstitious—who was the most superstitious guy in baseball, and he said, 'That crazy kid in Cleveland,' which was me. It got around so much that, one time when I was stretching before a game, one of my buddies tackled me and everybody came over and touched me, but I couldn't touch them back because they were holding me down. Another time I was on second base and the shortstop came over, touched me and got away before I could touch him back. That really bothered me at the time.

"It got to be pretty crazy. Fans were sending me things in the mail. Once I got a shirt that had a hand printed on it and it said, 'This constitutes a touch, and I got you last!' Another time (clubhouse attendant) Cy Buynak called me to the phone and said there was a guy on the line who said that talking with me constituted a touch. Crazy things like that. A magazine even wanted to do a story on it.

"I finally forced myself to quit it when I realized my kids had become aware of what I was doing. We were in a shopping mall and they started making left turns in order to make a right turn. That's when, when my family started getting involved in it, I figured it was time to end it."

Eddie Robinson

(First baseman, 1942, 46-48, 57)

On July 6, 1947, Larry Doby joined the Indians as the first black player in the American League, and the second, to Jackie Robinson, in major league baseball. Between games of a double header against the White Sox in Chicago that day, Indians manager Lou Boudreau told Doby he would play first base in the second game, which upset regular first baseman Eddie Robinson.

"Boudreau walked over to me and said, 'Hey Eddie, I want to borrow your glove. Doby is going to play first base," Robinson recalled. "He told me this after telling me a couple of days earlier, after I'd hit a couple of home runs, 'Don't worry, you're my first baseman.' Doby had never played first base. He was always a second baseman (in the Negro League). Joe Gordon would have been happy not to play, but here Boudreau was taking me out of the lineup after telling me not to worry.

"I said to Lou, 'You can have my glove and my uniform, too. I'm quitting,' and remained in the clubhouse the first three innings, intending to shower and dress in street clothes and leave the clubhouse, when (coach) Bill McKechnie came in.

"(McKechnie) said, 'Eddie, I know what this is all about. I know what's going through your mind. But what you and I know, it's not going to come out that way in the paper. It's going to look like you're doing this because of Doby being black. We know that's not the case, but it's not going to look that way in the paper. It's in your best interest, and for your future to put your uniform on and come back out (to the field).'

"So I did, and that was it. The end of it, and McKechnie was right."

Frank Robinson

(Outfielder, designated hitter;
Manager, 1975-77)

Upon being introduced as Major League Baseball's first black manager, and the 28th manager of the Indians on October 3, 1974, Frank Robinson said, "If I had one wish I was sure would be granted, it would be that Jackie (Robinson) could be here, seated alongside me today."

On the first day of spring training in 1975, Robinson was being interviewed by the three beat writers covering the Indians that year: Bob Sudyk of the *Cleveland Press*, Hank Kozloski of the *Lorain Journal*, and Russell Schneider of the *Cleveland Plain Dealer*.

Kozloski asked Robinson a question and, in answering, the manager called Kozloski "Russ." Kozloski said, "No, I'm Hank," and pointed to Schneider, saying, "He's Russ."

Robinson smiled and said, "Oh, OK, all you guys look alike."

Having played most of his Hall of Fame career with the Baltimore Orioles, Robinson was accustomed to winning. But the Indians hadn't won a pennant since 1954, and a World Series since 1948, to which Robinson quipped, "Pennant fever in Cleveland is a 24-hour virus."

In his inaugural season as manager of the Indians, Robinson had numerous battles with umpires, and on July 8, prior to a game in Oakland, he "rated" the arbiters in a newspaper story, which earned him a hefty fine by American League President Lee MacPhail.

In his evaluation, Robinson said that only ten of the 24-man umpiring staff was "creditable," 13 were "less than creditable," and that he had not seen enough of the one remaining member to express an opinion.

Twenty-six years later, in 2001, Robinson was appointed "vice president for on-field operations" by Commissioner Bud Selig, and one aspect of his job was to assess penalties against players who were overly aggressive in their complaints against umpires.

Rich Rollins

(Third baseman, 1970)

"There was a game in Boston one night in 1970 that I'll never forget, even though I didn't play in it—which is the reason I'll never forget it.

"Ted Uhlaender was our center fielder, and the fans in the bleachers at Fenway Park started throwing things at him, probably because we were winning and they were mad at us, and Ted was the closest to them.

"Anyway, they started peppering Ted with bottles, batteries, all kinds of things, and finally he ran off the field and into the clubhouse. The game had to be held up because we didn't have anybody in center field, and Uhlaender flat-out refused to leave the clubhouse. He said, 'I'm not going to subject myself to that kind of abuse, because nobody is doing anything about it.' The cops, if there were any out there, just let the fans do what they wanted.

"The problem was that Alvin Dark, our manager, had nobody else to put in center field. No other outfielders at all, and the umpires were threatening to forfeit the game unless we got somebody—Uhlaender or somebody, *anybody* out to center field right away.

"Well, Alvin figured that, because I'd been Ted's teammate in Minnesota for seven or eight years, I could talk him into going back on the field. So I went into the locker room and said to Ted, 'C'mon, Alvin has nobody to put out there. Go back out there or they'll forfeit the game.'

"Finally he said, 'OK, I'll go back to the dugout, but I won't go out to center field unless I see a policeman up there (in the bleachers) every 10 or 20 feet in that front row. And if I don't see cops out there, I'm not staying on the field.'

"So, with that, the Red Sox made sure enough security people were stationed in the bleachers, Ted went back to center field and the game resumed.

"The reason it was so important to me was that Alvin had told me that if Uhlaender wouldn't go back in the game, I'd have to be the center fielder—and I never played the outfield in my life."

John Romano

(Catcher, 1960-64)

"After I was traded by the Indians (with Tommy John and Tommie Agee) to Chicago (for Rocky Colavito) in 1965,

I hit a home run over the center field fence off Luis Tiant my first trip to the plate (in a game in late-July). The next time I got up we had men on second and third and, with first base open, the proper strategy was to walk me. But Birdie Tebbetts wasn't about to put me on, not after trading me away.

"(Catcher) Joe Azcue kept looking over toward the dugout and asking, 'Should we walk him?' but Birdie just pointed to the sky and yelled, 'Don't walk him . . . he's gonna pop up.'

"Well, I didn't pop up, I hit another homer, this one for three runs. But even that's not the best part of the story, though it's the part I like to remember best.

"In the seventh or eighth inning (White Sox manager) Eddie Stanky brought in relief pitcher Hoyt Wilhelm, a guy I never caught before. So, as soon as they announced him, I walked over to the dugout and started taking my stuff off, my chest protector and shin guards, and Stanky said, 'What are you doing? Where are you going?' I said, 'I don't catch knuckle ballers,' and he said, 'Tonight you are.'

"What happened next—and this is the part I'll never forget, though I'd like to—Wilhelm struck out the first three guys he faced, but all of them reached, loading the bases, because I couldn't catch the third strike on each of them. After each one I looked into the dugout, and Stanky just motioned me back to the plate.

"We finally got out of the inning and I went into the dugout and started throwing my mask and shin guards around. Stanky, sitting on the top step of the dugout, said to me 'Now what are you doing?' and I said, 'Tell me, how do you catch this guy?"

"Well, somehow I did. The game went into extra innings, and I never missed another pitch from Wilhelm. I couldn't believe it. Neither could Wilhelm—or Stanky.

"Did we win the game? That part I don't remember."
(The White Sox won, 9-4)

Al Rosen

(Third baseman/first baseman, 1947-56)

Recalling the pressure-packed end of the 1948 season, when the Indians finished in a tie with Boston for first place in the American League, Al Rosen said, "After we lost the last game (to Detroit), forcing a playoff game in Boston the next day, believe it or not, just about everybody was half in the bag on the train going to Boston that night.

"But it didn't bother those guys (his teammates). Nothing did. They were like the Three Musketeers, you know, one for all and all for one, except there were more than three; there were a lot of them.

"On the train to Boston, each table in the dining car had champagne and three or four bottles of booze on it. The whole thing was amazing. It was like everybody knew we were going to win. No sweat. I'd never seen anything like it.

"After I went to bed, Gene Bearden woke me up about one o'clock and asked me, 'Did you ever play first base? I said, 'No,' and he said, 'Well, you're playing first base tomorrow.' I got cold chills, I couldn't sleep the rest of the night. As it turned out, Bearden was wrong. I didn't play first base, Allie Clark did, and it probably was a good thing that I didn't."

Al Rosen

Rosen almost won the Triple Crown in 1953 when he led the American League with 43 homers and 145 RBI, but his .335559 batting average (rounded off to .336) was .001612 behind Mickey Vernon's .337171 (rounded off to .337).

"In the last week of the season I went to (manager) Al Lopez and said, 'I need at-bats, would you mind letting me lead off?' We were out of the race by then and Al said, 'If you want to do it, it's OK with me.' So I hit leadoff the last four or five games, and it worked out well because I was hot and getting a lot of hits. But so was Vernon.

"We went into the last game (against Detroit) and the first time up (Tigers third baseman) Ray Boone was playing back and, knowing I had to do something radical and different to catch Vernon, I laid down a bunt. The first one in my life. Never in the history of the game did I beat out a bunt—before or after. But I did this time, and was credited with a hit. The next time up, I doubled over the right fielder's head and got another hit later, so I was 3-for-4 going into my last trip to the plate. At the same time we were listening to what Mickey Vernon was doing in Washington and knew that he had two hits in four times at-bat, meaning that I needed another hit to beat him.

"Al Aber, a left-hander who was a little on the wild side, was pitching for the Tigers when I batted for the fifth time. He was trying to get the ball over the plate but just couldn't, and I kept fouling balls off, even though they weren't strikes, because I didn't want to walk. One of his pitches actually nicked me on the arm, and I yelled, 'foul ball, foul ball,' and the umpire went along with it, because everyone knew what the situation was.

"Finally I hit a high chopper to third base—though it also would have been ball four if I had taken the pitch— and I tried my darnedest to beat it out. My last step was a leap for the bag like a runner trying to reach the finish line, but I came up just short, and umpire Hank Soar called me out.

"Of course our bench erupted, claiming I was safe—and there are people I still hear from who say I was safe—though I knew I was out. Lopez came out to argue with Soar, but I told him, 'Al, I was out. (Soar) called it right,' and that was the end of it, and Vernon won the batting championship.

"I look back and think how great it would have been to win the Triple Crown, because there haven't been too many guys who have done it, but it didn't happen, and I've never dwelled on it. It's just one of those great stories that I like to tell."

Rosen worked for George Steinbrenner in 1978 and part of 1979, but for only a year and a half. "I had problems with George, and George had problems with me," he said. "My problem was that George was too dictatorial. He gave me responsibility, but not authority, and probably was the biggest second guesser I ever met in my life. A very difficult man to work for.

"And yet, I could probably call George Steinbrenner right now and say, 'George, I need $100,000,' and he'd probably not say a word and send a guy with the money.

"But working for him, and being his friend are two different things. That's what I said when I left (resigned) the Yankees in July 1979. I said, 'George, I'd rather be your friend than work for you.'"

During Rosen's tenure as president of the Yankees, they finished the 1978 season in a tie with the Red Sox for the pennant, and it was Rosen who made the call of a coin flip that determined where the one-game playoff would take place.

"I was in the American League office, and Haywood Sullivan (then general manager of the Red Sox) was on the phone. I told him, 'You call it, Sully,' but he said, 'No, you're right there, Al, you call it because you can see it.' George, of course, wanted the game in Yankee Stadium.

"Well, we lost the coin flip, and I had to call George and tell him. He asked me, 'What did you call?' I told him, 'Tails,' and he said, 'Dammit! What do you mean you called tails? Don't you know that the probable odds are that heads comes up more often?' "

As it turned out, the Yankees won the game, 5-4, on a home run by Bucky Dent, who hit only four home runs all that season.

Hank Ruszkowski

(Catcher, 1944-45, 47)

The Indians had high hopes for rookie Hank Ruszkowski, a Clevelander who was their opening day catcher in 1945, and played in 14 games that season before he was drafted and spent the next two years in the Army. He returned to play 23 games for the Tribe in 1947, but missed most of 1948 with a shoulder injury that required surgery.

Upon reporting to spring training in 1949 Ruszkowski had a theory that he believed would make him a powerful long ball hitter, though then-manager Lou Boudreau vehemently disagreed.

As reported by Ed McAuley in the *Cleveland News*, Ruszkowski checked in with an assortment of new bats that weighed 48 ounces. At the time, the heaviest bat in the major leagues was one that weighed 44 ounces swung by muscular Johnny Mize.

Ruszkowski was quoted by McAuley as saying, "Babe Ruth used a 54-ounce bat, and Riggs Stephenson (a .336 hitter who played in the major leagues from 1921-34) swung 56 ounces. I know I'm strong enough to use a 50-ounce bat, and I think it will give me more power to all fields."

Ruszkowski's theory: "Most hitters use an unnatural and unnecessary motion when they bring their bat from their shoulder at the start of their swings. The only part of the swing that counts is the level sweep through the ball. So why not start the swing in that plane, instead of doing so with the bat on the hitter's shoulder?"

Boudreau didn't agree and tried to convince Ruszkowski to use the orthodox style, but the catcher refused. Finally the manager issued an ultimatum, and when Ruszkowski maintained his stubborn attitude, insisting upon proving his theory, he was demoted to the minor leagues and never got another chance with the Indians, who released him on May 3, 1949.

Chico Salmon

(Infielder/outfielder, 1964-68)

Although his versatility was his strength—he played every position for the Indians except pitcher and catcher—Chico Salmon hated to be called "Super Sub," according to Dino Lucarelli, then of the team's publicity department and later its public relations director.

But the fact is, it was Salmon's versatility that enabled him to play nine years in the major leagues, the last four (1969-72) with Baltimore.

When he came to the Indians, Lucarelli said, "A story appeared that said Chico believed in ghosts, which is why, he said, he slept with the lights on in his bedroom. But everybody thought it was just a ploy so that Chico wouldn't be required to have a roommate, as did everybody else on the team in those days.

"One night he went on the 'Sportsline' radio show with Pete Franklin, whom Chico always called 'Ben,' not Pete. Franklin tried to get Chico to admit that the ghost story was a hoax. 'Let's disprove it once and for all,' Franklin said. 'You don't really see ghosts, do you, Chico?'

"Chico replied, 'Tha's right, Ben. I no sees 'em . . . but I believes in 'em.' "

Another Lucarelli story about Salmon:

"One winter Chico wanted to get an off-season job and stay in Cleveland. I contacted some people and found out that Stroh's brewery was looking for a celebrity representative. I arranged a luncheon with five or six Stroh's executives to come in from Detroit to meet Chico. We sat down and everything was going great. We laughed a lot and the Stroh's people seemed to like Chico. Then the waitress came over to take our order and when she asked Chico what he wanted to drink, he said, 'I gonna have a Budweiser.'

"He did not get the job."

Jim Schlemmer

(Sportswriter, Akron Beacon Journal)

When he covered the Indians, which he did for 45 years until his retirement in 1969, Jim Schlemmer was noted for his critical, often sarcastic comments about the team's players, coaches, managers and front office personnel.

He spared nobody, and nobody was invulnerable to Schlemmer's acerbic barbs, not even fellow sportswriters.

But the rotund and balding Schlemmer also was a character and, when the occasion presented itself, a hard drinker as well. Which was the case one night in Tucson, Arizona during the Indians spring training in 1964. This time, however, what happened to Schlemmer was almost disastrous to a man of his position.

In his ground level room at the Highway House motel, Schlemmer imbibed too much—actually, *much* too much—one night after finishing his column and, after getting undressed for the purpose of taking a shower, he stepped through the door to his right that he thought led to the bathroom.

However, it was the door to Schlemmer's left that led to the bathroom. The door to his right, which he opened and walked through—and which slammed shut behind him —led instead to the parking lot. Suddenly Schlemmer, sans even his underwear, found himself in the parking lot, locked out of his room.

Fortunately, there was some shrubbery that he was able to hide behind, which he did for nearly two hours while fighting off mosquitoes and other assorted bugs that frequented the desert. Finally, with the clock approaching 2 a.m., a friend—well, a colleague who worked for a competing newspaper and on occasion was the butt of Schlemmer's acerbity—came along.

Schlemmer caught the man's attention and pleaded with him to obtain a spare key. The man finally did, but not until after he tormented the naked sportswriter from Akron who, thereafter, always made sure of the door he walked through, and/or was fully dressed before doing so.

Herb Score

(Pitcher, 1955-59)

In spring training 1957, after Herb Score had won 36 games and lost 19 his first two seasons with the Indians, Hall of Famer Tris Speaker, then a member of the Indians front office, said, "If nothing happens to Score, the kid has got to be the greatest."

Less than a month later, on May 7, Score was hit in the right eye by a line drive off the bat of the New York Yankees Gil McDougald, and didn't pitch again that season. Though he recovered from that injury, Score was never the same and retired in 1962 with a career won-lost record of 55-46.

After he became a broadcaster of Indians games, first on television and then, on radio, Herb quickly became as big a favorite of the fans in his new capacity, as he was when he wore a uniform and toe plate, and struck out opposing batters.

Listening to Herb was like sitting next to a friend and watching a baseball game with his down-home style. He wasn't always perfectly articulate and, to be sure, he often was guilty of a *faux pas*. But nobody objected, as when he committed one of his—nay, one of the fans'—favorite comments during what was considered "the bad old days" of the 1980s.

When an Indians' batter hit a drive down the left field line, Score excitedly shouted into the microphone, "It could be fair, it could be foul . . . it is!"

But, again, the fans loved it, as they loved Score.

Phil Seghi

(General Manager, 1973-85)

Prior to Frank Robinson's first game as player-manager of the Indians—and Major League Baseball's first black manager—on April 8, 1975, against the New York Yankees, he was visited in the clubhouse by Indians General Manager Phil Seghi.

Seghi said to Robinson, "Frank, why don't you hit a homer the first time you go to the plate?," to which Robinson responded, 'Are you crazy, or what?'

An hour or so later, as the Indians' second batter to face Yankees right-hander Doc Medich, Robinson homered, leading the Indians to a 5-3 victory.

Mark Shapiro

(Assistant General Manager, 1998-00, General Manager, 2001-)

"The day we traded Sean Casey is one of the more memorable days in my time with the Indians. I was farm director when John Hart and Dan O'Dowd made the (1998) deal with Cincinnati (for pitcher Dave Burba). They asked my opinion, and I told them I couldn't be objective and shouldn't be involved in the decision. I could never trade Sean Casey, even though we desperately needed Burba.

"And, while I shared Sean's happiness, because he was going to get an opportunity that we both knew wouldn't happen here, I was simply too attached to him. I felt absolute sorrow because he was one of the very special people I'd ever been around, but wasn't going to be a major leaguer in a Cleveland uniform.

"So, we both were in tears as we shared some great discussion, and it was the basis for a friendship that still exists today.

"The bottom line is that it was a good deal, one of those deals that was good for both clubs. Burba provided what we desperately needed at that time by winning 15 games three straight years (1998, 1999, 2000), while Casey has become one of the best players in the National League."

"My favorite memory (since joining the Indians in 1992) involved Tony Peña in Game 1 of the 1995 Division Series against the Red Sox. It was Yom Kippur, so I wasn't there (at Jacobs Field). I shouldn't even have been watching the game on TV. When Peña hit that home run in the 13th inning (that won the game, 5-4) it set the tone for a magical postseason."

In addition to Peña's game-winner, Shapiro also treasures the memory of Sandy Alomar's game-winning homer off New York Yankees closer Mariano Rivera in the 1997 Division Series. It sent the Indians on their way to their second World Series appearance in three years. "We were five outs from elimination when (Alomar) got that home run off the best relief pitcher in baseball," he said. "It symbolized hope for the team. It's etched in the minds of all our fans."

Sonny Siebert

(Pitcher, 1964-69)

"Sam McDowell and I were roommates and lockered next to each other most of the time. I used to listen to him being interviewed after games, and I never knew if he was kidding you guys, the way he'd answer your questions, when you'd come around to interview him after a game.

"One of the things he'd do was, when Bob Sudyk (of the *Cleveland Press*) would ask him, for example, what kind of a pitch he threw to strike out the last batter, Sam would say, 'Fastball.'

"Then, after Sudyk would leave and you (Russ Schneider of the *Cleveland Plain Dealer*) would ask him the same question, Sam would say it was a curveball.

Sonny Siebert

"Then it would be Hank Kozloski's (of the *Lorain Journal*) turn to ask what pitch he threw to get the last out and Sam would say, 'change-up.'

"It amazed me. I had trouble keeping a straight face when I'd hear him do that. Once I asked him why, and Sam said, 'Oh, you know those guys. They all want something different, so I give it to them.' "

"The thing I remember so well about my no-hitter (2-0 over Washington, June 10, 1966) is similar to the time I came close to pitching a second no-hitter (for Boston five years later).

"Joe Azcue was my catcher with the Indians and, at the start of the ninth inning, he was a little nervous. He didn't want to do anything to spoil the no-hitter. When the first batter came to the plate, Joe got down in his crouch and put his fist down three times in a row without putting down any fingers.

"I called him out to the mound and asked him what was going on, and he said he didn't want to call for the wrong pitch. I told him I'd been throwing mostly fastballs, let's stay with it, which we did.

"I retired the first two batters without any trouble, and got two quick strikes on the third batter, Rabbit Saverine. He started to swing at my next pitch, but held back. Before the umpire ruled that he hadn't swung and that it wasn't strike three, everybody in our dugout jumped out on the field, and everybody in the stands started cheering.

"It took about ten minutes to get all our guys back in the dugout and even some fans off the field, and I thought for sure I'd lose the no-hitter. But then Saverine hit a routine fly to left, and that was it. I got the no-hitter.

"Then, in 1971, when I was with the Red Sox, almost the same thing happened. I took a no-hitter against the Yankees into the ninth and my catcher, Tom Satriano, came out and asked me, just as Joe did, how I wanted to work the hitters. I thought back to 1966 and told him the same thing. That I'd better stay with fast balls, even though, by then, I wasn't throwing as hard as I had a few years earlier.

"So what happened? The first pitch I threw to the first batter, Horace Clarke, was a fast ball. He hit it up the middle and there went my no-hitter, so it didn't work twice in a row.

"Like somebody once said, sometimes you can think too much."

"At one time I thought, when I got out of baseball and became a businessman, I'd probably have to go by my given first name, Wilfred, instead of Sonny. I mean, when somebody named 'Sonny' reaches middle age, as I have, how can he still be called Sonny?

"But I don't know. I still get mail addressed to 'Sonny Siebert,' and I even get checks—most of them are small checks now—that some are made out to 'Sonny' and sometimes 'Wilfred,' so I guess it doesn't really make any difference. And my family and my friends still call me Sonny.

"Actually, I'm the third Wilfred in my family, which might be the reason I've always been called Sonny. My grandfather was the first Wilfred, though everybody called him Charley, but don't ask me why. Then, my father was the second Wilfred and people call him Joe, and I don't know the reason for that, either.

"So, there are three Wilfred Sieberts in my family, but none of us is called Wilfred, at least not all the time."

Duke Sims

(Catcher, 1964-70)

"I always got a kick out of Luis Tiant, and I loved to catch him. He was a very funny man, even when he got mad. One time, I guess it was about 1966, Looie was pitching, I'm catching and the umpire behind the plate was Frank Umont, who had a bit of a drinking problem at that time. It was a hot and very muggy day in Cleveland, Umont was sweating like hell and didn't smell too good. Everything he drank the night before was coming out.

"Looie, who always had great control, was throwing strikes, but Umont kept calling them balls. Looie got all bent out of shape and when I got back to the dugout I went to (manager) Birdie Tebbetts and asked him, 'Birdie, am I doing something that would keep Umont from calling the pitches right?' Birdie said, 'No, I've been watching and you're not doing anything wrong. Umont is just horse (bleep), that's all.' Then Birdie said, 'The next time Looie throws a pitch that's a strike and Umont calls it a ball, you look into the dugout, and then I want you to go to the pitcher's mound.'

"So, we went back on the field and a couple of pitches later, Looie threw one right down Broadway, and Umont called it a ball. I looked into the dugout at Birdie, as he told me to do, then I called time and walked out to the mound. Looie was beside himself, he was so mad. I told him, 'Looie, look, Birdie is on his way out here, so I'm just killing time until he gets here. Don't worry about Umont. He's just having a tough time.'

"When Birdie got there he told Looie to look in at the plate at Umont and tell him when Umont was coming out (to break up the conference). So, we didn't talk, we just stood there, Birdie and me with our backs to the plate, and waited for Umont to come out. When Umont did, he said, 'OK, Birdie, what's going on? You going to make a change?'

"With that, Birdie turned around and looked me right in the eyes and said, 'And you, Sims, you get one more good pitch from Tiant called a ball, I'm going to fine you five hundred bucks.' Then he turned around and walked off. Tiant started to chuckle, and I went back to the plate with Umont right behind me. When we got there, Umont said, 'Boy, Birdie sure is tough on you, ain't he?' and I said, 'No, Frank. Birdie was talking to you.' He said, 'Really?' and I said, 'Really.'

"And after that, for whatever reason, Umont got better—and Tiant won the game."

Joel Skinner

(Catcher, 1989-91; Coach, 2001-)

"We were playing in Cleveland—I was with the Yankees then, I think it was 1988—and Richie Yett was pitching for the Indians. We had a man on third and Lou Piniella gave me the sign for a squeeze bunt. When I tried to lay it down, Richie pitched out, but didn't get it out quite far enough. I was able to reach out with one hand and bunt the ball down the first base line and got the run in.

"After they threw me out at first base, I circled around to the right and ran back to the (third base) dugout. As I went past the Indians dugout, I saw Doc Edwards, then the Indians manager, raise his right hand and punch the clipboard he was holding something awful. Pieces of it went flying all over the dugout, which made it even greater for me, knowing that it frustrated him so.

"I laughed about it later, though I never brought it up to Doc, which was a good thing because the next year I was playing for him (in Cleveland)."

C. C. Slapnicka

(Scout/General Manager, 1935-41;
Scout, 1946-70)

In a meeting with the Indians directors in the spring of 1936, C.C. Slapnicka, the team's head scout, said, "I suppose this sounds like the same old stuff to you, but I want you to believe me. This boy I found out in Iowa will be the greatest pitcher the world has ever known. His fastball is fast and fuzzy, never goes in a straight line, it wiggles and shoots around."

Slapnicka was talking about Bob Feller.

Pat Tabler

(Outfielder/Designated Hitter/
First baseman, 1983-88)

"One thing that stands out in my memory from the years I played in Cleveland was the excitement of the fans, especially in 1986 when we went on a ten-game winning streak.

"After we won No. 10 in Chicago, we heard on the plane ride home how excited the fans were back in Cleveland. The next night, when we played Kansas City, the game had to be delayed for 20 to 30 minutes to let all the fans get through the gates. There were about 50,000 fans in the Stadium that night and, I'm telling you, it was very exciting—and different. The first three years I was with the Indians we were losing close to a hundred games each season, and not doing well at the gate.

"But in 1986 all my friends were calling me for tickets, and I had a huge pass list that night we came back to Cleveland to play the Royals. We went into the bottom of the ninth with the score tied, and when we loaded the bases, the Royals brought in Dan Quisenberry. I went up and got a hit that won the game, and I'll never forget the excitement that was generated, the way the fans went crazy.

"Like Gabe Paul said that Cleveland was a sleeping giant and that, if they ever had a really good team, the fans would really support the Indians, really get into it, which is what's happened. I think it's great.

"The following winter (1986-87) we were on the cover of *Sports Illustrated* with the prediction that we were going to win the pennant in 1987—and the knuckle-headed reason was that five or six years in a row, a different team had won the American League East. So *S.I.* figured it was our turn, because we had a young, up and coming team.

"But we really stunk it up, finished last (with a 61-101 record). It had been great to get the national recognition, but a lot of us knew we were a young team, and the sad truth was, we just weren't ready. We were not a complete team. Not then. Not against the Yankees and the Red Sox and the Orioles and the Brewers. Detroit ended up winning the division."

"One of the reasons we did so well for awhile in 1986, when we led the major leagues in hitting, was that any way it was possible to steal the catchers' signs, we did. Doc Edwards (then a coach) was in the bullpen, stealing the signs and relaying them to the hitters. That was right after we'd switched bullpens from right field to left field, the (publicized) reason being that (manager) Pat Corrales could then see better from our (first base) dugout who was throwing in the pen.

"It started the night we were playing Baltimore and Doc discovered that (Orioles shortstop) Cal Ripken would hold his bare hand a certain way behind his back, depending on what pitch was being called, to let the outfielders know what the pitch would be so they could get a better jump. A closed fist was a curve ball, and an open fist was a fast ball. Doc would raise his right hand in the air for a fast ball, and lower it for a breaking ball. I think we scored, like, 15 runs that night (actually ten) and, I'll tell you, it's great hitting when you know what's coming. Left-handed batters at the plate could see Doc, but the signal had to be relayed from somebody in the dugout for right-handed batters. If it was a fastball, somebody in the dugout would whistle, and if it was going to be a curveball, somebody maybe would yell out the batter's name. Not everybody wanted to know, but I sure don't know why not. I did, that's for sure."

Ed Taubensee

(Catcher, 1991, 2001-)

"It wasn't the most embarrassed I've ever been in baseball, but, yeah, it was pretty embarrassing," acknowledged Eddie Taubensee, talking about the only time in major league baseball history that a pitcher pitched both right-handed and left-handed in an official game.

The ambidextrous pitcher was Greg Harris, a natural right-hander who was on the mound for Montreal against Cincinnati on September 28, 1995. In the sixth inning, Reggie Sanders, a right-handed batter, led off, and was followed by left-handers Hal Morris and Taubensee.

Harris retired Sanders on an infield grounder, then, switching his glove to his right hand he pitched left-handed and walked Morris. Then it was Taubensee's turn to face Harris. "I took his first two pitches, which were slow fastballs . . . maybe 70, 75 miles per hour," said Taubensee. "Then I hit his third pitch—I think it was supposed to be a fastball, too—off the end of my bat, right back to (Harris), and he threw me out at first base.

"When I got back to the dugout, the guys were laughing. They got a big kick out of it," said Taubensee. "But, what the heck, it was no big thing"—even though it never happened before, or since in the major leagues.

Birdie Tebbetts

(Catcher, 1951-52; Manager, 1963-66)

In 1952, when the Indians, then managed by Al Lopez, signed Herb Score out of high school in Lake Worth, Florida, Birdie Tebbetts was a back-up catcher (with Joe Tipton) behind Jim Hegan. The Indians brought Score to Cleveland for a workout before they sent him to the minor leagues. Mike McNally, then the farm director, told Score, "Don't throw hard until you get good and loose, and let us see what you've got," according to a tale told by then-manager Al Lopez.

Score was throwing to catcher Birdie Tebbetts when Lopez approached the young pitcher and introduced himself. Lopez stood behind the mound and, a few minutes later, asked Score if he was ready to "cut loose." Score said, "Yes, that's what I've been waiting to do," and Lopez told him, "Go ahead, but don't hurt yourself."

With that, Score said to Birdie, "Mr. Tebbetts, I'm going to let it out now," and the veteran catcher said, "You mean you haven't thrown hard yet?" Score said he hadn't, whereupon Tebbetts yelled to Tipton, "Hey, Joe, c'mon over here and catch this kid. I'm the next hitter (in batting practice)."

Tipton dutifully took Tebbetts' place and told Score, "OK, kid, let it come," which Herb did. His first pitch, a fastball, went over Tipton's head without the catcher even getting a glove on it. Lopez said, "Tipton turned pale because he knew if the ball had hit him, it would've got him right between the eyes, maybe even killed him. With that,

Tipton yelled at Birdie, 'Tebbetts, you son of a bitch, you almost got me killed,' which was true.

"Then Tipton got down in a catcher's crouch and told Score to throw another pitch. Herb did, it was a curveball, and this one broke down and hit Tipton on the instep of his left foot. Now Tipton is really mad at Tebbetts. He threw down his glove and limped away. Hegan had to come out and finish catching Score, while Tebbetts hid behind a couple of players at the batting cage."

However, it was another left-handed pitcher who impressed Tebbetts even more. "Sam McDowell was the greatest talent I ever saw, period. There was none better, not Herb Score, not Bob Feller, not Bob Lemon, not Early Wynn, not anybody, anywhere. He threw as hard as anyone, he had a great curve ball, a great slider and a great change-up - and he also had a spit ball. But, like a lot of guys, he didn't know how to use his talent. He wasted it. He just couldn't put it all together."

Andre Thornton

(First baseman/designated hitter, 1977-79, 81-87)

"Something I learned early on, and was driven home to me many times, is that baseball is a game that teaches humility. I know it did to me. You play the game the way it's supposed to be played, and you don't get too cocky out there, because one minute you're up on cloud nine, and the next minute you can be humiliated in front of 30 or 40 thousand people.

"Like the time we were playing in Boston and I was swinging a pretty hot bat. First base was open and (Red Sox manager) Don Zimmer intentionally walked the batter ahead of me. I got a hit and drove in a run, and when the inning ended, I went out to first base and was thinking, 'Who is Don Zimmer to walk a batter in order to pitch to me?'

"The next thing that happened, there was a pop-up between first and second base. I thought Duane Kuiper would catch it, and he thought I would, and the ball fell between us. It scored a run and immediately brought back to me a sense of humility."

"Humility can come in another form, too. Like the night my wife Gail sang the National Anthem prior to a game at the old Stadium in the late 1970s. We were playing the Yankees and afterwards Yogi Berra came up to me and said, 'Andre, your daughter'—he called Gail my daughter—'did a great job.'

"When I told Gail, she liked it, of course, though it made me think it might be time to retire."

"The day I hit for the cycle in 1978, the thing I remember most is that I went into Boston struggling like a dog as I was off to my usual slow start at the plate. I don't recall the sequel of the hits I got, although I remember the triple came in my last at-bat. People ask me, how in the world did I ever get a triple—although I wasn't all that slow.

"What happened was that the ball I hit almost went out of Fenway Park, and would have if it hadn't been to center field where the wall comes to a point. The ball ricocheted off the wall and away from the outfielders so that I was able to make it to third base easily.

"Another thing people kid me about is the game in which I hit an inside-the-park home run, the only time I ever did that. We were in Chicago, and Richie Zisk, the left fielder, for some reason was playing me over toward left center. Steve Stone was pitching for the White Sox, and that was the day in 1977 that Kuiper hit the only home run of his career.

"I hit a towering pop fly down the left field foul line and when it came down it almost hit the chalk, out near the warning track. Zisk was so far away from the line that he couldn't get there, and—I guess because it had rained earlier in the day and the ground was wet—he couldn't stop. By the time he did, I was on my way home. But if it had been anybody other than Richie Zisk out there, I never would have gotten to home plate because he was slower than I was."

Luis Tiant

(Pitcher, 1964-69)

"When I got called up by the Indians (from Class AAA Portland on July 19, 1964) I did not want to go. We were in San Diego and I was supposed to pitch that night. They canceled me, but didn't tell me why. The next day (Portland manager) Johnny Lipon called me into his room and told me, 'You have to go to New York. The Indians want you.'

"I said, 'No way. I don't want to go.' He asked why, and I told him, 'Because they waited for me to win 15 games

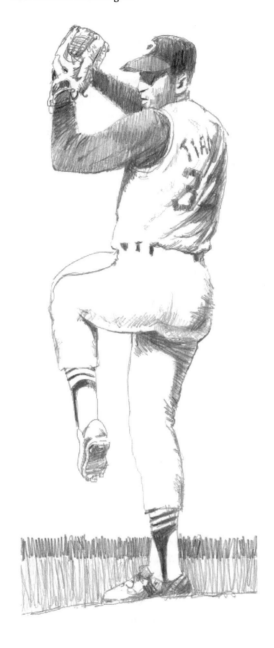

Luis Tiant

(with only one loss at Portland). Why didn't they call me when I was 8-0? Sam McDowell was 8-0, and they called him up, but not me.' Lipon said I had to go. 'This might be your only chance, so you better go now.'

"I left San Diego at 7 o'clock at night and arrived in New York at 7:30 the next morning. When I got to my room at the hotel I got a call from Gabe Paul. He said, 'Come to my room to sign a new (major league) contract. It was for $5,000. The minimum salary that year was $6,000, but they only gave me $5,000 because it was July, not the start of the season.

"When I went to the ball park that night (manager) Birdie Tebbetts asked me how I felt, if I was ready to pitch. I said I was ready, because I was supposed to pitch (in San Diego) the night before. He said, 'OK, you are pitching tomorrow.'

"I pitched good, struck out 11 and we won, 3-0 (which tied the record for a rookie pitcher throwing a shutout in his first game in the big leagues). People couldn't believe it. I was too happy to be tired. It was a good feeling, especially because it was against the Yankees. That was the last year they won the pennant (until 1976).

"Yogi Berra was the Yankees manager then and after the game he said in the paper that he knew me, that he faced me before, once in Cuba, and that I was pretty old.

"But it wasn't me. He batted against my father (Luis Sr.). That's why he thought I was real old. But I was only 23 (in 1964). My father pitched in Cuba for about 24 years. Everybody who used to play with him in winter ball said he was very good. They would tell me, 'Looie, you are good, but your father was better.' "

"One of the craziest things I did in a game was a time in 1967 against Boston. Reggie Smith was on second base, and I was pitching to George Scott. I wanted to pick Smith off, but at the same time I wanted to pitch to Scott. So I stepped off the rubber and started to turn to second base, but instead I threw the ball home. I was all messed up. I guess I did it, because after I set up (in a stretch position), I saw Reggie take a walking lead off second.

"Scott was so surprised he didn't know what to do, and started yelling, 'What's he doing? Is he crazy?' Nestor Chylak, the umpire, didn't know what to do either. Or what to call. He said, 'What the hell are you doing?' I said, 'I don't know. That never happened to me before,' and he said, 'All the years I have been in baseball I never saw anything like that.'

"Finally Chylak called it a balk. He told (manager) Birdie Tebbetts, 'I have to call it something, and I don't know what else to call it, so it's a balk,' because, when I made the pitch, my foot was not in contact with the rubber. But he also told us, if Scott had swung at the ball, he would have been out. Don't ask me why. That's all Chylak said. The whole thing was crazy, but I won the game, so it was OK.

"And if one of my players ever does what I did, I don't know what I'd say either."

Tiant was the baseball coach at Savannah (Georgia) College of Art and Design.

"My baseball team did not do good this year (2000). We were bad. It reminded me of when I was in Cleveland (in the 1960s) and we couldn't beat nobody. Maybe I was a bad coach. I don't know. But I don't think I will be there no more. They have a new president, and he did not offer me a new contract."

Bill Veeck

(Owner, 1946-49)

On June 22, 1946, the Indians were purchased for $2 million by Bill Veeck, who built them into a World Series championship team in 1948. Veeck spent a great deal of time in the stands, mingling with fans, and said, "I have discovered in 20 years of moving around a ball park that the fans' knowledge of the game is usually in inverse proportion to the price of the seats they are occupying."

On July 3, 1947, Veeck purchased the contract of Larry Doby for $10,000 from the Newark Eagles of the Negro National League. Two days later, Doby became the first African-American to play in the American League and second (by 11 weeks to Jackie Robinson) in the major leagues.

Several years later, in recalling Doby's first time at-bat for the Indians as a pinch hitter against the Chicago White Sox on July 5, 1947, Veeck related the following in a national magazine:

"He swung at three pitches and missed each by at least a foot. (Doby) was so discouraged . . . he sat in the corner (of the dugout), all alone, with his head in his hands. Joe Gordon was up next . . . and missed each of three pitches by at least two feet and came back to the bench and sat down next to Doby, and put his head in his hands, too."

It was a nice story that Veeck told, but the fact is, Gordon was on third base when Doby batted, as reported in a book about Doby entitled, *Pride Against Prejudice*.

Other Veeck-isms: "Baseball is almost the only orderly thing in a very unorderly world. If you get three strikes, even the best lawyer in the world can't get you off."

"I try not to break the rules . . . merely to test their elasticity."

"We didn't win the pennant in 1948. We won it on November 25, 1947, the day I rehired Lou Boudreau (as manager of the Indians)."

Mickey Vernon

(First baseman, 1949-50, 58)

"The best thing about being traded to the Indians (December 14, 1948) was that I won't have to bat against Bob Feller, Bob Lemon, Gene Bearden. It should add at least 20 points to my average (because) instead of facing the Indians, I'll be batting against Washington pitching."

(A year later he was traded back to Washington.)

Omar Vizquel

(Shortstop, 1994-)

"When I was growing up (in Venezuela) Davey Concepcion was my idol, and I always wanted to be a ball player. But when I went to a tryout camp, they told me I was too small . . . that I should go to the racetrack and be a jockey."

On April 16, 1994, prior to a game against the Kansas City Royals at Jacobs Field, Vizquel was asked by a reporter about his defensive prowess, after he'd won a first Gold Glove award while playing shortstop for Seattle in 1993. "I would like to go an entire season without making an error . . . which is not impossible," he said.

An hour or so later, during a 12-9 loss to the Royals, Vizquel was charged with three errors, his first of the season, but still went on to win another Gold Glove in 1994, and every year through 2001, for nine straight.

Leon Wagner

(Outfielder, 1964-68)

Though unhappy about the 25-percent cut in salary that Gabe Paul proposed in 1967, Leon Wagner said, "I've got too much pride to hold out for more money after the kind of season I had (in 1966). The way I look at it, I'm like a racehorse . . . you've got to win or place to collect the big money. I just showed."

Rick Waits

(Pitcher, 1975-83)

"One of the funny things I remember about my career is that my first day in the major leagues, when I was with Texas before I was traded to the Indians, I had three managers within a 24-hour period.

"I was called up by the Rangers in September (1973) after I'd gone 14-7 and won the Triple-A championship game (for Spokane of the Pacific Coast League). Whitey Herzog was the Texas manager then and said he was going to give me a start. But three hours later, at about 5 o'clock, Herzog was fired, and the Rangers made Del Wilbur, who'd been my Triple-A manager, the interim manager. I figured I'd surely get in some games, because Wilbur knew me from Spokane. But right after that first game, the door to the clubhouse flew open, and here came a bunch of TV cameras following Billy Martin, who'd just been named the new manager of the Rangers, my third manager in less than 24 hours.

Under Billy I pitched only one inning in that final month, and got a save. But that's all. No starts, as Whitey had promised, or as I expected to get with Wilbur.

"As it turned out, that was the only inning I ever pitched for the Rangers. They sent me back to the minor leagues in 1974, and I was still there (until June 13, 1975) when the Indians traded Gaylord Perry to Texas for Jim Bibby, Jackie Brown and me, and cash. I heard it was $250,000, because there always was a lot of money involved in deals the Indians made in those days.

"After that a lot of great things happened to me in Cleveland. At the time we—Bibby and Brown and I—thought it was a tough trade for Cleveland to make, giving up their best pitcher for three young guys and cash. But one thing the three of us remember—and we always kept track of it—is that the three of us always combined to win more games for Cleveland than Gaylord did for Texas."

"Playing for Frank Robinson was good. He gave me the ball. He gave me the chance to pitch, which Texas never did, even though I had won at every (minor league) level I played. That first half-year with Cleveland in 1975 was great. I was 6-2 with a two-something (2.96) ERA, and I'll be forever thankful to Frank for giving me the chance.

"But that's not the only reason I thought Robinson was a great manager. Remember, we did not have a real great ball club those seasons (1975-77), and when he was fired (June 19, 1977), I thought it was way too soon to pass judgment on him. At the time we were playing pretty decent ball, but had just gone into a little spin. I think they made the change just for the sake of change when they gave the job to Jeff Torborg.

"Jeff was a great friend, he'd been my bullpen coach and changed some things that made me a better pitcher. But still, I thought Frank knew the game as well as anyone. He was a tough guy, very aggressive, and nobody liked to win more than Frank Robinson—even when he played a game of cards—and I enjoyed pitching for him. I sure did."

Bill Wambsganss

(Second baseman, 1914-23)

If ever a man was in precisely the right place at precisely the right time, it was Bill Wambsganss, better known in baseball history as Bill Wamby.

Wamby's right place at the right time was about three strides to the right of second base at Cleveland's old League Park in the fifth inning of the fifth game of the World Series against Brooklyn, October 10, 1920.

Because he was, Wambsganss was able to make the only unassisted triple play in World Series history, helping the Indians win the game, 8-1.

"You'd have thought I was born the day before and died the day after. The only credit I deserve is for being in the right place at the right time," Wambsganss said. He speared a line drive off the bat of Willie Mitchell, his momentum carried him to second base, where he doubled Pete Kilduff, and then turned and tagged Otto Miller, who was running from first.

"After the game I was interviewed by one newspaperman. A guy from Brooklyn talked to me. He asked me how it felt to make an unassisted triple play. I said it was the chance of a lifetime, which it was," Wambsganss said.

Jim Warfield

(Trainer, 1971-)

"In my 30 years as a trainer for the Indians, I've had a lot of 'favorite' players, so don't ask me to name my most favorite. There are too many. But one of them is Gaylord Perry, who also goes down in my book as one of the classiest, most dedicated, professional, conscientious, and hardest workers I've ever been around, in baseball or anywhere.

"The mention of his name brings back a memory that I'll never forget; it took place during the 1974 season. That was not a good year for the Indians, though it certainly was for Gaylord, who went on to win 21 games.

"But it was a game he didn't win that I remember so well. It was played on July 8 in Oakland, with the A's on their way to a third straight World Series championship. Gaylord went into the game with 15 consecutive victories, needing one more to tie the American League record (held by Smoky Joe Wood, 1912; Walter Johnson, 1912; Lefty Grove, 1931; and Schoolboy Rowe, 1934).

"Something else that made all those victories by Gaylord even more impressive was the fact that many of the 15 games—in fact, the last six or seven in a row—he won while pitching with a badly sprained right ankle that nobody knew about. He didn't want the press to find out because, if they wrote about it, he was afraid opposing batters would bunt on him, and he probably was right.

"Vida Blue pitched for the A's against Gaylord that night and, even though it was a Monday and the game wasn't scheduled to be televised back to Cleveland, the station sent a crew to Oakland to cover it; it was that big back home.

"Oakland scored first on a two-run homer by Gene Tenace (in the second inning) and was ahead, 2-0, until we scored in the fifth and went ahead, 3-2, in the seventh when Dave Duncan hit a two-run homer. But Oakland tied it, 3-3, in the ninth, and won in the tenth (on a walk, sacrifice bunt, and pinch hitter Claudell Washington's first major league hit, a single to left)."

"Gaylord was great, but Blue was just as tough against us, and retired the last ten batters in a row (through the top of the tenth), after Duncan's homer. That's how Gaylord's winning streak was stopped."

But that didn't end Warfield's story.

"After the game, as I always did, I cut the tape off Gaylord's ankles, took off the hot applications and cream that he used on his arm, and helped him with some shoulder exercises, then he went in and took his shower. Through it all, Gaylord never said a word, and he still didn't when he came out of the shower, and we did some more shoulder work, as we always did. When I was finished, he just got up off the table and walked out, still without saying a word.

"The next day Gaylord came to the Coliseum about 11 o'clock in the morning with his son Jackson and said to me, 'Pardner,' which is what he always called me, 'there was a reason I didn't say anything to you after the game last night. It's because that was the toughest defeat of my career, and I just didn't want to talk about it. I hope you understand.' Of course I did."

Fred Weisman

*(Oldest son of Lefty,
the Indians trainer from 1921-49)*

"Because of my dad, my brother Jed and I were sort of celebrities growing up in Cleveland Heights in the 1930s and 1940s, though we didn't think it was anything special to have players coming to the house almost every night. At that time most of the games were played in the afternoon and some of the Indians often would drop in and sing with my dad, while I played a few chords on the piano for them.

"I liked all of the guys, but I'd have to say my favorites probably were Jim Hegan, Joe Vosmik and Earl Averill. My dad made us call all the players 'Mister,' never by just their first name, which was a lesson I learned early. Once I called Vosmik 'Joe,' because he told me I should. But when my dad heard me, 'Boom!' he whacked me across the back of my head and told me to watch my manners. I always did after that.

"In 1936, when I was nine, they let me be the batboy, and I made an eastern trip with the team. That was the year Bob Feller joined the Indians at the age of 17, and he and I would go out together after games. We had to be in bed in our room by nine o'clock, and by nine the next morning we'd be at the ball park throwing and running together. It was great. Those were some of my fondest memories."

Jed Weisman

(Youngest son of Lefty Weisman)

"When I was born (in 1933), Alva Bradley, then the owner of the Indians, suggested to my dad that I be named for the team's starting outfielders, who were Joe Vosmik in left, Earl Averill in center, and Dick Porter in right. So my name, Jed, was a combination of 'J' from Joe Vosmik, 'E' for Earl Averill, and 'D' for Dick Porter.

"I'm often reminded how lucky I was to be named Jed, because, at that time, another outfielder named Bob Seeds was fighting Vosmik to be the starting left fielder. If he had won the job, my name might have been 'Sap,' for Seeds, Averill and Porter, instead of Jed. I guess I should always be thankful that Vosmik was better than Seeds."

"I enjoyed being around the players, and my greatest memory probably goes back to 1948 when the Indians took me on a western swing, to Detroit, Chicago and St. Louis. Before one game, I think it was in St. Louis, while the Indians were taking infield practice, Lou Boudreau called me out on the field and told me to take ground balls at shortstop while he went into the clubhouse. Imagine that! They let me do everything except take the catcher's throws at second base—they probably thought I'd miss the ball and maybe get hurt—but I did pretty well, if I do say so myself.

"As my brother Fred said, we weren't allowed to call the players by their first name, although one day Steve Gromek said to me, 'Either you call me Steve, and not Mr.

Gromek, or I'll call you Mr. Weisman and not Jed.' So I did, but never around my dad."

Dr. William Wilder

(Indians team physician/medical director, 1970-00; medical consultant, 01-)

"If anybody ever wondered about how stressful it can be to manage a major league baseball team, I can relate a couple of instances that will prove that it is very stressful, beginning with Ken Aspromonte (who managed the Indians from 1972-74) and continuing with his successor, Frank Robinson (1975-77).

"In the case of Aspromonte, he never knew what was going on in the front office, as neither Gabe Paul nor Phil Seghi talked much to him. One day Kenny called me to say that he was very concerned about his looks. He was losing the hair (whiskers) on his face. It was very embarrassing to him. I examined him and found no sign of an infection, or that anything was (physically) wrong. All I could tell him was that sometimes something like that happens when you are under a great deal of stress—which he really was at that time. Things were not going well with the Indians, and they certainly didn't get any better when, unknown to Aspromonte, the Indians acquired Robinson (in mid-September 1974 from California).

"Aspromonte found out about it when he walked into the locker room for a ball game and there was Robinson, putting on a uniform. It was right after that that

Aspromonte's wife Laurie came to our house and borrowed our typewriter to type Kenny's resignation speech that he gave to the players.

"At that time Robinson had this big Afro hairdo, which wasn't as large as Oscar Gamble's, but it was big. A few months into Robinson's term (in 1975) he called me into his office at the Stadium one night and said, 'Doc, you've got to look at my hair. I'm getting holes in my hair.' His hair was coming out, the same as Aspromonte's did, and all I could say to him was, 'Frank, you've got Aspromonte's disease. It happens because of stress. Call it the 'Manager's Syndrome.' "

"Those were crazy days. Things were happening that were really crazy involving several of the players, the 'rat pack,' we called them. They did some wild things off the field, and some of the bus rides were . . . well, really turbulent. That's all I should say about it.

"All that's kind of funny now, as I told Robinson last year at the winter meetings when he was named vice president for on-field operations, or as you guys (in the media) call him, the 'Czar for Discipline.' As I said to him then, 'Frank, you did everything off the field that was wrong, that you shouldn't have done, so you should know what all these guys can get into.' He said, 'Shhh, don't tell anybody.' "

"Something else I remember so well about Robby, after his first season as manager of the Indians. He had rotator cuff surgery that October (1975) and after the operation I got a call from the hospital that he was having an irregular heartbeat. I went in to see him in his private room, but I could hardly examine him because he was watching the World Series on television and didn't want me to get in his way. It was a case of first things first, you know.

"It (Robinson's irregular heart beat) didn't seem to be a major problem, but I felt it would be best if he was moved to the Intensive Care Unit where his heart could be monitored. He looked at me and asked, 'Do they have TV down there?' I told him no, and he said he wouldn't go because he wanted to continue watching the World Series. So we had to round up a (heart) monitor to put in his room, because he refused to go to the Intensive Care Unit where he couldn't watch the game on television."

Stan Williams

(Pitcher, 1965, 67-69)

"I pitched for Los Angeles (1958-62) and the New York Yankees (1963-64) before I went to the Indians, and when I was with the Dodgers in the winter of 1960-61, I had a contract problem with (general manager) Buzzie Bavasi. He argued that I walked too many guys and, because I did, he was refusing to give me the $2,500 raise I wanted that would have jumped my salary up to $10,500.

"Buzzie said, 'Tell me why I should I give you a $2,500 raise,' and I told him, 'Because I'm going to do these five things for you: First, I'm going to walk fewer than 75 batters, I'm going to pitch 230 innings, win 15 games, strike out 200 batters, and have an ERA under 3.00. Buzzie said, 'That's fine. But don't just tell me you're going to do it, do it and I'll pay you.'

Stan Williams

"As it turned out, I made three of them; I won 15 games, pitched 235 innings, and struck out over 200 batters (205), though my ERA was a little more than 3.00, and my walk total was over 75 (108), so I didn't get the $2,500.

"But I tried hard, especially to keep from walking a lot of guys. Anytime I'd get behind in the count on a batter, like 3-and-0, or 3-and-1, I just went ahead and drilled the s.o.b. because nothing was said about HBPs (hit batters).

"But I couldn't do enough of it. Word got around about what I was doing, and guys got harder for me to drill.

"And, no, Buzzie never did give me the $2,500."

"Of all the games I pitched in the big leagues (482) one of my best, maybe the best, was in 1967 (August 10). The Indians had brought me back after I'd had a sore arm and had been out of the big leagues for almost three full seasons.

"We were in Baltimore, and Sonny Siebert was supposed to start, but he told (manager) Joe Adcock he needed one more day. So Adcock asked me if I could pitch and I told him, 'That's what I'm here for.' I started the game and went all the way, 13 innings, and won, 2-1.

"The reason it's one of my favorites is because I struck out two Hall of Famers nine times—Luis Aparicio five times and Frank Robinson four times.

"The first three times Robinson batted, I struck him out on a fastball, the second time with a curve, and the third time with a slider. The fourth time he came up I got him 0-and-2 and I'm thinking, 'What is he sitting on? What should I throw him?' I'd already struck him out on a fastball, curve and slider.

"Then it occurred to me that I hadn't thrown him a spitball—and I had a good one. So I turned my back to the plate, loaded one up and threw him a helluva spitter, low and away. He swung and missed it by about two feet.

"Imagine that. There I am, a guy who'd had a bad arm and was out of the big leagues for three years, who came back and threw a 2-1 victory, went all 13 innings, struck out 15 and just pitched a helluva game.

"But the next day the headline in the paper was, 'Robinson accuses Williams of throwing a spitter'—even though that one was the only one I threw the whole game."

Rick Wise

(Pitcher, 1978-79)

"There have been a couple hundred no-hitters in the history of major league baseball. But mine, when I beat Cincinnati, 4-0 (June 23, 1971) was the only one of its kind, because I also hit two home runs in it. I'm in my own company, and that makes it very special to me."

"It was difficult for me when I was traded to Cleveland from the Red Sox during spring training of 1978 and I had to join the Indians in Tucson (Arizona). I'd had some very good years in Boston. We had gone to the World Series in 1975, and I'd had some personal highs while I was there, although, at the time I was kind of on the outside looking in with Don Zimmer (the Red Sox manager). He'd shuffled some of the pitchers between the starting rotation and the bullpen, and back again, so I wasn't really surprised when the Red Sox traded me.

"But surprised or not, I was disappointed because Boston was a strong and contending club, and Cleveland wasn't. It also was disappointing to have to pick up and go all the way across the country for spring training without knowing my teammates, really not knowing anybody with the (Cleveland) club.

"The way the fans were in those days also made it difficult. It probably took ten games or so to put as many fans in the seats in Cleveland to equal what the Red Sox would get for one day, for just about every game they played.

"It also was difficult playing in Cleveland, because the Stadium then was really a football stadium, not a baseball park like Fenway, or like so many parks today, including Jacobs Field. We'd need 80,000 to fill the stadium, but we'd be lucky to get six or seven thousand for a game in July and August.

"But I've got to say that the guys on the Indians, to their credit, played as hard as they could, no matter the problems. It's just that, for the most part their talent level was not as good as the rest of the league, though we had some outstanding individual players. We just couldn't put it all together as a team. We didn't have the consistency you need to be a winner in major league baseball."

Early Wynn

(Pitcher, 1949-57, 63)

"There I was, getting out guys like Joe DiMaggio, King Kong Keller, Bill Dickey, Joe Gordon, Red Rolfe and Tommy Henrich, but I lose the game because that little pip squeak

(Phil) Rizzuto hit a home run," said Early Wynn, after a 1-0 loss to the New York Yankees on September 26, 1941. "From that game on, I always thought bad things about anyone who hit a home run off me."

In 1957, during Kerby Farrell's ill-fated season as manager of the Indians, he went to the mound to either replace or simply talk to Wynn. The gruff pitcher, who was not happy about the way the game was progressing, greeted the manager by saying, "What the hell do you want? Get the hell out of here. I can take care of this myself," whereupon Farrell turned around and dutifully returned to the dugout.

On another occasion, when Al Lopez managed the Indians (1951-56), he went out to get Wynn. It was Lopez's second trip to the mound that inning, which meant Wynn had to be replaced by a relief pitcher. Just as Lopez reached the mound umpire Bill Summers, who had been a target of Wynn's wrath, told the pitcher, "One more word out of you, and you're gone."

Then, according to Lopez, "Early looked at Summers, then at me, and said to Summers, 'Why the hell do you think (Lopez) is coming out here . . . to bring me a ham sandwich?' Early knew he was coming out of the game, so it didn't matter if he said another word or not."

Celebrate the Heroes of Baseball

in These Other Acclaimed Titles from Sports Publishing!